THE WONDERFUL WORLD
OF
AMERICAN ADVERTISEMENTS

1865·1900

These Belts are for sale at drug stores, but if not in your immediate vicinity, send direct to Dr. SCOTT, 842 Broadway, New York.

Each is stamped with the name Pall Mall Electric Ass'n of London.

AWAY WITH PHYSIC AND QUACK NOSTRUMS!

THE WONDERFUL WORLD OF AMERICAN ADVERTISEMENTS

1865 – 1900

LEONARD DE VRIES   ILONKA VAN AMSTEL

FOLLETT PUBLISHING COMPANY

CHICAGO

ACKNOWLEDGEMENT

The authors wish to acknowledge their gratitude
to the staff of the New York Public Library for their
hospitality and valuable help.

Second Printing

FOREWORD

With the Civil War decade, the United States was witness to a number of new, far-reaching developments in advertising techniques. The country's population was ever-hungry for war news, and this led to the birth of the special Sunday editions of the daily newspapers. This insured a much larger circulation for advertisers and, consequently, not only did old advertisers increase the size and scope of their ads, but new advertisers were quickly attracted by the circulation boom. The more skeptical merchants were finally convinced of the power of advertising, and it became a fact of life in American business.

Also invaluable to the rise of advertising was the advent of cheap paper, known as newsprint, and, in 1865, the perfection of a new type of printing press that enabled newspaper publishers to print larger papers with much greater speed and efficiency.

Along with the industrial growth of America came the rising importance of women and their purchasing power. Earlier, it had been customary for the men to do the family shopping and planning. But with the Civil War, more and more women were called upon to come away from their household duties and assume responsibilities as family planners. A woman's weekly trip to the nearest shopping area became part of her household routine, and merchants and advertisers soon began to reflect this change in their promotion and advertising.

Once women were recognized as important consumers, a new trend was started toward magazines and periodicals catering exclusively to women. Advertisers were quick to see the market possibilities, and artists and designers were called upon to use all their talents to capture the new audience.

During the postwar period, conditions led to extravagance and excess in many directions, and it is during this time that the heady, overly-ornate, elaborate and distorted advertisements started to grow in popularity. There seemed to be a race between advertisers to see which one of them could use the largest number of different styles of type, the most scroll work, the most angelic looking faces, and the smallest miniprint that enabled them to get the most linage out of their advertising space.

No consumer item was exempt from this ornamental race. Wheel chairs, corsets, kidney pads, photography equipment, chewing gum holders, soap, and furniture are but a few of the thousands of items advertised in this fashion during this period.

Also during the postwar period, the field of lithography began applying its talents to commerce and industry. Color lithography started to fill the demands for advertisements, magazine supplements, sheet music covers and billboard posters. It was in this period that the greatest advances were made in the use of outdoor billboards as an advertising technique.

But lithographers had great competition from printers using woodcut blocks. They devised large assortments of giant wood letters which, when combined with stock designs or specially made pictures, would fill the needs of the advertisers more economically.

With the Philadelphia Centennial Exposition in 1876, there was once again a huge boom in the numbers of newspapers and magazines published. At the Exposition itself, the public was brought face to face for the first time with the force of advertising. Throughout the halls, which were filled with exhibits and displays of new consumer products, were handbills, leaflets and flyers hawking the virtues of these new products.

It was then, also, that the newly-created mail-order business rapidly grew, creating an instant need for catalogs, price lists, and advertising flyers. It soon became clear that pictures sold goods most effectively, and the wood engravers soon began to supply this need with their cold and factual illustrations.

Advertising illustration soon turned away from those cold and factual days, and at the very end of the nineteenth century, the overly-ornamental and elaborate advertising style, popular ever since the end of the Civil War, reached its peak.

Presented here, in retrospect, are many of the most popular advertisements of the period from 1865 to 1900. They provide the reader with an exciting, first-hand look at the styles and the tempo of the time. While modern technology has advanced at an astounding pace, these advertisements will also present the reader with an alarmingly accurate idea of how far our tastes have not progressed.

THE PUBLISHER

CONTENTS

HEALTH

C HAMPION SPRING MATTRESS—The latest and best improvement. Do you want a healthy and comfortable bed? Here it is. The softest, easiest, cheapest, most popular, and durable Spring Bed in market. Sold by all leading dealers. No stock complete without it. Wholly composed of tenacious tempered steel springs, so united that the pressure is equally distributed. Easily moved or carried about the house. Can be lifted, turned, or rolled up like a blanket. Both sides alike. No frame, no wooden slats, no straps. May be used on floor without bedstead. No under bed required. Needs only half thickness of hair mattress. The regular size double bed, 4 ft. 6 in. by 6 ft., contains 192 steel upholstery springs and weighs only thirty lbs. More springs for your money in this bed than in any other. Warranted noiseless. Any sizes made to order Send for pictorial circular. Retail price of double bed, $13. Shipped, by single bed or quantity, to all parts of the world. Liberal discount to the trade. Agents wanted. F. C. BEACH & CO., Makers, 102 Chambers St., cor. Church New York.

**All Deformities permanently cured by Dr. J. P. MANN,
No. 133 West 41st St., New York   Send for Circular.**

EPILEPSY OR FITS

A SURE CURE for this distressing complaint is now made known in a Treatise (of 48 octavo pages) on Foreign and Native Herbal Preparations, published by Dr. O. PHELPS BROWN. The prescription was discovered by him in such a providential manner that he cannot conscientiously refuse to make it known, as it has cured everybody who has used it for Fits, never having failed in a single case. The ingredients may be obtained from any druggist. A copy sent free to all applicants by mail. Address Dr. O. PHELPS BROWN, 21 Grand St., Jersey City, N. J.

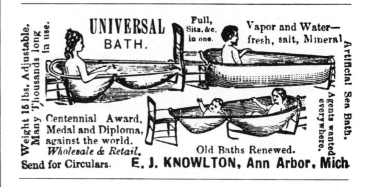

UNIVERSAL BATH. Full, Sitz. &c. in one. Vapor and Water—fresh, salt, Mineral

Weight 15 lbs. Adjustable. Many Thousands long in use.

Centennial Award. Medal and Diploma, against the world. *Wholesale & Retail.* Old Baths Renewed.

Artificial Sea Bath. Agents wanted everywhere.

Send for Circulars.   E. J. KNOWLTON, Ann Arbor. Mich.

World's ONLY Manufacturer of
WHEEL CHAIRS
EXCLUSIVELY. ALL STYLES and SIZES for **Invalids and Cripples.**
Self-propulsion by use of hands only in street or house. Comfort, durability, and ease of movement *unequalled.* Patentee and Maker of the "Rolling-Chairs" pushed about at the Centennial. For Illustrated Catalogue send stamp, and mention *Youth's Companion.*

HERBERT S. SMITH, 32 Platt Street, N. Y.

Laboratory of P. H. Drake & Co., New York.

CRUSHING CALISAYA BARK &C. — TANK ROOM — PRESS ROOM — FILTERING ROOM — PREPARING PRINTED MATTER — PREPARING BOTTLES — PACKING ROOM — FILLING BOTTLING & LABELING — ADVERTISING DEPARTMENT — WARE-ROOM — RUM VAULT — ENGINE ROOM

THE UNPRECEDENTED GROWTH OF THE BUSINESS OF MESSRS. P. H. DRAKE & CO., of New York, is one of the wonders of this enterprising country. But a few years ago these gentlemen commenced the manufacture of the now celebrated PLANTATION BITTERS and MAGNOLIA WATER, in a common barrel, in an obscure location. The reputation of the articles spread faster than their ability to supply orders. There was hardly a nook or a corner of the civilized world which did not bear evidence of their enterprise and presence. Hogsheads gave way to tanks, single rooms to whole buildings, the hand-press to steam-engines. Material became exhausted. One agent was dispatched to South America to procure Calisaya; another to the West Indies to manufacture St. Croix Rum; while most of the Shaker brethren were engaged preserving roots and herbs. The above is a photographic sectional interior view of their present Laboratory, at 105 and 107 Liberty street, New York. The value of the buildings, fixtures and material on hand, is not less than $300,000. Near one hundred hands and several teams are kept employed. They pay the press near $100,000 per annum; and their total receipts are about the same as those of the New York and New Haven Railroad. It is useless to say such results could exist without merit. Viva la PLANTATION S. T. 1860, X!

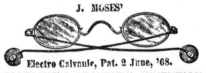
8/1865–1875

Hercules Supporting Corset.

The Latest and Most Improved Abdominal Corset.

Patented November 19, 1878.

No. 1, Sewed.................................$2.00
No. 2, Woven, Spoon Steel.............. 2.75

It supports the abdomen naturally. It cannot stretch It gives relief to invalids, and is a perfect-fitting Corset in every respect.

For sale by all first-class dealers in the U.S., or Samples sent on receipt of price by

LEWIS SCHIELE & CO.,
SOLE MANUFACTURERS,
NEW YORK.

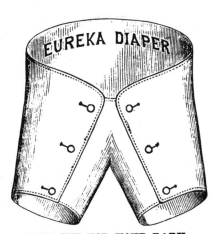

GET ONE FOR YOUR BABY.

EVERY baby must have it. Is thoroughly water-proof, protects clothing, retains linen diaper, avoids pins, permits circulation of air. Recommended by physicians and all mothers whose children have worn them. Made in 4 sizes—1, smallest : 4, largest—exclusively by EUREKA DIAPER CO., 532 Broadway, N.Y. Sample mailed on receipt of $1. Sold also by A. T. STEWART & Co., LORD & TAYLOR, and all first-class Infants' Clothing, Fancy, and Dry Goods Stores. Ask for Eureka Diaper ; see they bear stamp of Eureka Patent Diaper Co. Take no other.

Dr. D. Mac Rae,
CONSULTING AND OPERATING
SURGEON AND PHYSICIAN.

Treats all forms of chronic diseases, namely: Nasal Catarrh. Diseases of the Throat, Lungs, Heart, Liver, Stomach, etc., etc. Diseases of the Throat and Lungs are successfully cured by Inhalation of Atonized Vapor, etc. Rheumatism, Neuralgia, Paralysis, Skin Disease, Scrofula and malignant Ulcerations are cured by the Electro Chemical and Medicated Baths, etc.

CANCER      **CANCER**

Cancerous Tumors, Cancerous Ulceration, Cancer of the Womb. Spurious Growths, Tumors of all kinds ; also, Fistula and Pi es, successfully treated and cured without pain or use of knife, etc. Office No. 155, South Clark-st. *P. O. Box,* **814,** *Chicago, Ill.*
y1   D. MAC RAE, M. D.

For Cleansing the Teeth.

A NEW PRINCIPLE!   A NEW WAY
that Will Cure Throat and Lung Diseases.
DR. J. H. McLEAN'S
COUGH AND LUNG-HEALING GLOBULES.

This wonderful remedy will cure *Coughs, Colds, Asthma, Consumption,* and *Lung Diseases.* There is no mistake about it,

They are Sugar Globules !

DIRECTIONS: Take one Globule every two hours. Suck it until it is all dissolved. As rapidly as the saliva acts on the medicine it produces a healing gas, which you inhale ; and it is that medical gas which cures Consumption, Asthma, Bronchitis, or any disease or soreness in your Throat or Lungs. Try them and be convinced. Trial Boxes, 25 cents by mail. Full Boxes, also sent by mail, $1.00. They contain six times more than the Trial Boxes.

BEFORE TAKING.   AFTER TAKING.

DR. J. H. McLEAN,
314 CHESTNUT STREET, ST. LOUIS, MO.

Dr. J. H. McLEAN'S
CELEBRATED CATARRH SNUFF.

This remedy will cure Catarrh in all its forms. It is a remedy which can be used with Dr. J. H. McLean's Cough and Lung-Healing Globules where any *Bronchial* irritation exists. I know that any person afflicted with Catarrh has more or less Bronchitis.

For any *Soreness in your Throat, Swelled Tonsils, Inflammation or Ulceration in your Throat.* Try it, and you will be convinced of its *wonderful* virtues. I have relieved enlarged Tonsils in two hours by filling a quill or tube with Dr. J. H. McLean's Celebrated Catarrh Snuff and blowing it back on the inflamed parts, having them suck two or three of Dr. J. H. McLean's Cough and Lung-Healing Globules.

I therefore urge all who may have any soreness in the nose or throat to snuff at least once each day some of Dr. J. H. McLean's Celebrated Catarrh Snuff. Beware of (douching) snuffing up the nostrils salt water or any kind of water or picking the nose. They are all injurious. If your nose is stopped, keep trying until you get some of this Catarrh Snuff up in the nose in contact with the soreness, and you will soon feel its healing influence. Be sure to draw it up good, until you taste the powder in your throat. Try it! Dr. J. H. McLean's Catarrh Snuff. Trial boxes, 50 cents, by mail.

BEFORE TAKING.   AFTER TAKING.

DR. J. H. McLEAN,
314 Chestnut Street, ST. LOUIS, MO.

MR. MURRAY, of the "Golden Rule," writes: "I was troubled last Winter with an obstinate catarrh, which invaded my throat and lungs, and caused a most trying cough. I have used your medicine with *perfect success,* every trace of cough and catarrh having been removed by your truly wonderful remedy."

For the cure of Catarrh, Asthma and Lung Diseases we charge $5 for the first month's treatment, which consists of one bottle of Air, one of Balsam and one Inhaler. Every succeeding month $4. Our Cough Balsam $1 per bottle ; trial bottle, 50c. The medicine sent to any address C. O. D. Pamphlet, with particulars and testimonials, sent free. All letters must contain a 3c. stamp.
Dr. J. D. Judge & Co., 79 Beach St., Boston, Mass.

HOLMAN'S
Fever and Ague and Liver Pad
CURES WITHOUT MEDICINE, SIMPLY BY ABSORPTION.
The Best Liver Regulator in the World.

The only true cure for, and preventive of malaria, in all its forms :
Liver Complaint, Jaundice, Dyspepsia, Rheumatism, Yellow Fever, Sea-Sickness, Neuralgia, Bilious Disorders, &c., &c.

None genuine without the Trade-Mark and Signature of the Inventor on the wrapper.
Ask your druggist for it. For Certificates, read little blue book, *Enemy in the Air.*

TRADE-MARK.
Sent by mail on receipt of $2.
WM. F. KIDDER & CO., Sole Proprietors,
No. 83 John Street, N. Y.

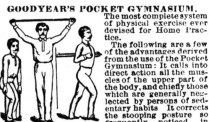
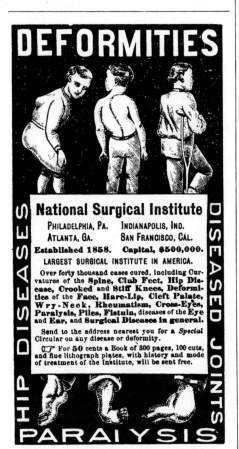
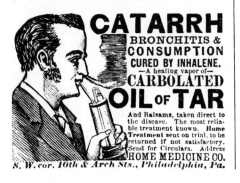

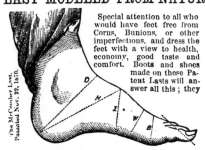
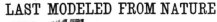

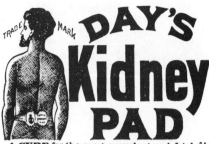

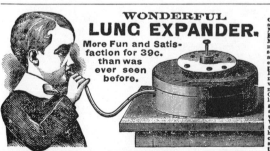

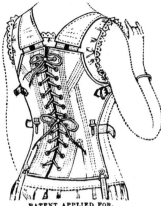
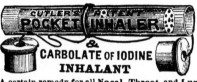

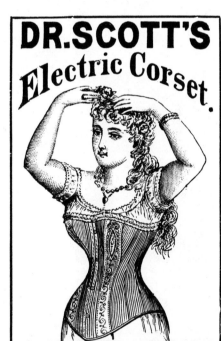

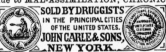

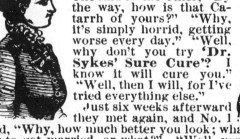

A Home Gymnasium.

Making over 20 combinations. Gifford's apparatus supplies a want long felt, and brings within the reach of every thinking person the means of acquiring a thorough physical education. Wall apparatus, $15; with rowing attachment, $5 extra. Complete Gymnasium, $30 and $35.

Send stamp for special Price-List of Gymnasium supplies.

A. G. SPALDING & BROS.,

108 Madison St., Chicago.

KNOWER INVALID HAMMOCK
FOR THE RELIEF OF THE SICK OR DISABLED.

Applied to any Bed, for following purposes:
1—To facilitate cleanly, easy use of commode or bed-pan without removal of patient from bed
2.—To change from reclining to sitting posture
3.—To raise patient to change bedding, and, 4—To prevent heating or bed sores. Send for circulars with testimonials to

A. M. LESLIE SURGICAL INSTRUMENT CO., ST. LOUIS MO.
Or W. P. KEATING, Room 275 Potter Building, New York.

PHYSICIANS RECOMMEND THE
"WILSONIA" MAGNETIC

CORSETS AND WAISTS FOR DAY OR NIGHT WEAR
On account of their Curative Properties.

A series of magnets scientifically arranged form minute batteries, recharging the blood with magnetism, without which life cannot exist, furnishing a wonderful remedy for Nervousness, General Debility, Indigestion, Rheumatism and Paralysis, the effect being exhilarating to the Wearer.

Get the Genuine. Price $3.00 & $12.00 per pair. Abdominal $15.00. We will send either style on receipt of price, which amount will be returned if not as represented. Send for descriptive catalogue, with Testimonials of Marvelous Cures.

THOMSON, LANGDON & CO., N. Y., SOLE MANUFACTURERS.

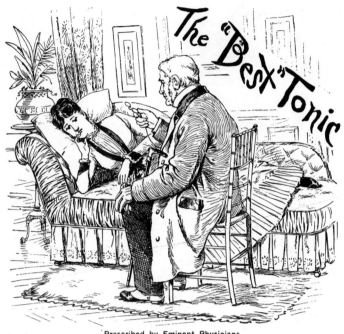

Prescribed by Eminent Physicians.

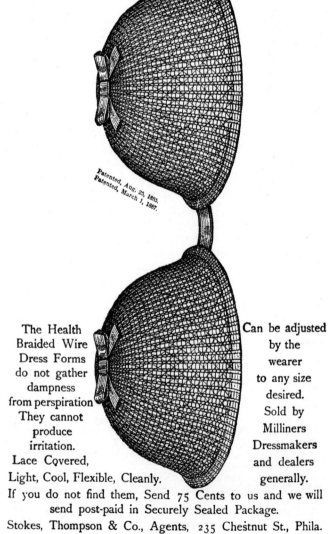

Patented, Aug. 25, 1885.
Patented, March 1, 1887.

The Health Braided Wire Dress Forms do not gather dampness from perspiration They cannot produce irritation. Lace Covered, Light, Cool, Flexible, Cleanly.

Can be adjusted by the wearer to any size desired. Sold by Milliners Dressmakers and dealers generally.

If you do not find them, Send 75 Cents to us and we will send post-paid in Securely Sealed Package.

Stokes, Thompson & Co., Agents, 235 Chestnut St., Phila.

THE HOME VAPOR BATH AND DISINFECTOR COMPANY,
12 East 23d Street, Madison Square, New York.

The following testimonials to the efficiency of the Home Vapor Bath will sustain what is claimed for it, that it is an important hygienic and sanitary improvement, ever ready to render valuable assistance in case of disease, and a luxurious comfort in one's own home. The apparatus, simple in all its appurtenances and in its operation, is made available to all, as it can easily be attached to any bath-tub in any dwelling provided with the ordinary hot-water kitchen boiler, without in any way interfering with the baths hitherto in use in our homes.

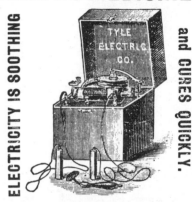
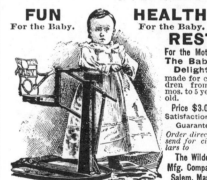

1682 or 1683? The date of PENN'S TREATY is in dispute, but it is universally admitted that Ayer's Cherry Pectoral prolongs and saves life, and therefore far exceeds, in value, anything that Penn ever offered the natives in exchange for their lands.

Mr. Wm. De Shaw, Port Madison, Wyoming Territory, writes: "While the Indians were holding a Grand Council here, recently, I distributed among them your Penn's Treaty cards, advertising Ayer's Cherry Pectoral. The dusky warriors were highly elated, and bought every bottle of the Pectoral I had in the store. Having tried it, they now know its curative powers, and no Indian thinks his outfit complete without a bottle of your medicine."

Ayer's Cherry Pectoral,

Prepared by Dr. J. C. Ayer & Co., Lowell, Mass. Sold by all Druggists.

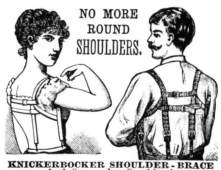
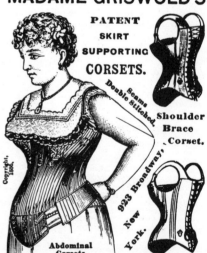
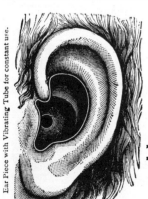

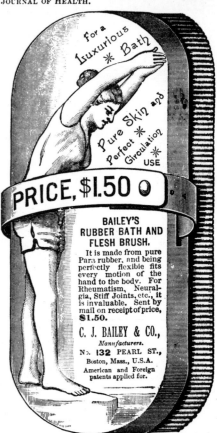
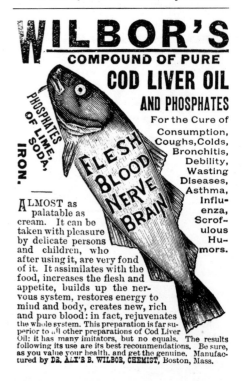

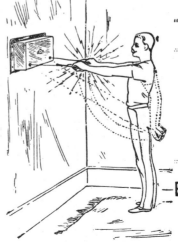

CUPID'S HARNESS.

Most women naturally look forward to matrimony as their proper sphere in life, but they should constantly bear in mind that a fair, rosy face, bright eyes, and a healthy, well-developed form, are the best passports to a happy marriage. All those wasting disorders, weaknesses, and functional irregularities peculiar to their sex, destroy beauty and attractiveness and make life miserable. An unfailing specific for these maladies is to be found in Dr. Pierce's Favorite Prescription. It is the only medicine for women, sold by druggists, **under a positive guarantee** from the manufacturers, that it will give satisfaction in every case, or money will be refunded. This guarantee has been printed on the bottle-wrappers, and faithfully carried out for many years. $1.00 per Bottle, or Six Bottles for $5.00.

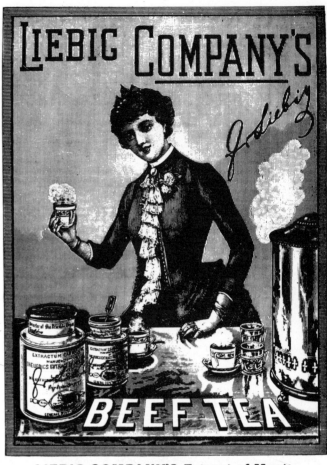

LIEBIC COMPANY'S BEEF TEA

LIEBIC COMPANY'S Extract of Meat
IS THE BEST.

It has a delicious flavor and dissolves clearly. Indispensable in good cooking, and invaluable as a healthful and refreshing beverage.

Get the *Genuine*, with *Justus von Liebig's signature* printed *in blue* on label, as shown on the picture above.

ARMS AND LECS
WITH THE NEW PATENTED
Rubber Hands and Feet.

MR. A. A. MARKS: SALINA, KANSAS.

Dear Sir: — After having worn one of your artificial legs with rubber foot for more than fifteen years, I have no hesitation in saying it is the best leg in use; as it is simple and the most durable of any I have seen. I have worn five different makes since 1862, and find none so useful as yours. I can heartily recommend the rubber foot as the most durable and easy to handle. I am a blacksmith, and shoe horses. I have dug wells and quarried stone, and other heavy work. I can walk farther in a given time than any man can on any other kind of a leg, with the same length of stump as mine; it is only three inches from hip joint.

Yours, etc.,

E. LINCOLN.

By our formula persons can supply us with all measurements necessary to secure a fit while they remain at home. Write for New Treatise of 430 pages with 246 illustrations.

A. A. MARKS, 701 Broadway, New York.

EYES TESTED FREE.

We guarantee to make Glasses that will prevent failing sight, and make weak eyes strong. Send stamp for test card, and find out what kind you need. Your old glasses put in gold bows for $3.50. Send them by mail.

KEENE OPTICAL CO.,
1301 Washington St. - Boston

MOTHERS! DAUGHTERS! SONS!
HEALTH AND STRENGTH

insured you your lifetime by using the "IMPERIAL 5 Pulley Exerciser" at home complete for $5.00. 1000 physicians recommend it. Book: Health and Strength in Physical Culture 40 ill. 5c. given with Exerciser. Ladies' book: An Ideal Complexion and Physi'l Development, 90 ill. 50c., or both books 75c. Chart of 40 Athletic cuts for Dumb Bells or Pulleys, 25c. Stamp for circular.

J. E. DOWD.
116 Monroe St., CHICAGO, ILL.

When ordering goods, please mention this paper.

WONDER CURE OF THE 19TH CENTURY
IMPROVED BATTERY
ONLY KNOWN CURE FOR CATARRH
U.S. REGISTERED LABEL "GENUINE" MUST ACCOMPANY EACH BATTERY.
STOPPER
COMPOUND PATENT
PATENT BATTERY
CURES CATARRH
RESTORES EYESIGHT
PRICE $10.00
Actinaleo
86 5TH AVENUE NEW YORK U.S.A.

SOLE PROPRIETORS AND MANUFACTURERS.

EAR Claxton's CAP, Patent.

For Remedying Prominent Ears. Prevents disfigurements in after life. Keeps the Hair from Tangling.

Sold in 3 Sizes, Nos. 1 and 3 for Infants. No. 5 for Children. Post Free for $1.50. A. Claxton, 62 Strand, London, England.

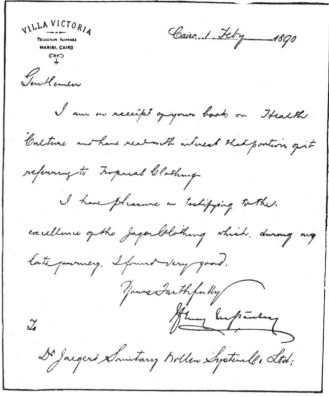

Mothers and Children

Everywhere bless the
Cuticura Remedies

WHEN SIX MONTHS OLD, the left hand of our little grandchild began to swell, and had every appearance of a large boil. We poulticed it, but all to no purpose. About five months after, it became a running sore. Soon other sores formed. He then had two of them on each hand, and as his blood became more and more impure it took less time for them to break out. A sore came on the chin, beneath the under lip, which was very offensive. His head was one solid scab, discharging a great deal. This was his condition at twenty-two months old, when I undertook the care of him, his mother having died when he was a little more than a year old, of consumption (scrofula, of course). He could walk a little, but could not get up if he fell down, and could not move when in bed, having no use of his hands. I immediately commenced with the CUTICURA REMEDIES, using all freely. One sore after another healed, a bony matter forming in each one of these five deep ones just before healing, which would finally grow loose, and were taken out; then they would heal rapidly. One of these ugly bone formations I preserved. After taking a dozen and a half bottles he was completely cured, and is now, at the age of six years, a strong and healthy child.

MAY 9, 1885.   Mrs. E. S. DRIGGS,
612 E. Clay St., Bloomington, Ill.
SEPT. 13, 1888. — No return of disease to date.
E. S. D.

I have been afflicted for a great many years with bad blood, which has caused me to have sores on my body. My hands were in a solid sore for over a year. I had tried almost everything I could hear of, but had given up all hopes of ever being cured, when I saw the advertisement of the CUTICURA REMEDIES. I used one box of CUTICURA, one bottle of RESOLVENT, and one cake of SOAP, and am now able to do all my own work.
Mrs. FANNIE STEWART, Staunton, Ind.

I have used the CUTICURA REMEDIES successfully for my baby, who was afflicted with eczema, and had such intense itching that he got no rest day or night; but after I had used two boxes, the skin began to peel off and get clear and soft. The itching is gone, and my baby is cured, and is now a healthy, rosy-cheeked boy.
MARY KELLERMANN, Beloit, Kan.

Your CUTICURA REMEDIES did wonderful things for me. They cured my skin disease, which has been of five years' standing, after hundreds of dollars had been spent in trying to cure it. Nothing did me any good until I commenced the use of the CUTICURA REMEDIES. Our house will never be without them.
Mrs. ROSA KELLY, Rockwell City, Calhoun Co., Ia.

Cuticura Remedies.

CUTICURA, the great skin cure, instantly allays the most agonizing itching and inflammation, clears the skin and scalp of every trace of disease, heals ulcers and sores, removes crusts and scales, and restores the hair. CUTICURA SOAP, the greatest of skin beautifiers, is indispensable in treating skin diseases and baby humors. It produces the whitest, clearest skin and softest hands, free from pimple, spot, or blemish. CUTICURA RESOLVENT, the new blood purifier, cleanses the blood of all impurities and poisonous elements, and thus removes the CAUSE. Hence the CUTICURA REMEDIES are the only infallible curatives for every form of skin, scalp, and blood diseases, from pimples to scrofula.

CUTICURA REMEDIES are sold by druggists and chemists throughout the world. Price: CUTICURA, 50 cents per box; CUTICURA SOAP, 25 cents; CUTICURA RESOLVENT, $1.00 per bottle. Prepared by POTTER DRUG AND CHEMICAL CORPORATION, Boston, Mass.

☞ Send for "How to Cure Skin Diseases," 64 pages, 50 illustrations, and 100 testimonials.

THE G=D BUST SUPPORTER

Allows healthy, natural development of the body.
PRICE $1.00
Made of finest Satteen in White, Gray and Black, and Summer Netting. Sizes 18 to 30 *waist measure.* At all leading dealers or sent to any address on receipt of price, post paid.
GAGE-DOWNS CO., Chicago

The Baby's Delight
Exercising Machine

The most practical, healthful and amusing device for children's use ever introduced. Very attractive to Baby, and invaluable for children backward about walking. If every mother knew how much labor it would save her, and how her baby would enjoy it, she would not be without it.
Price, $3.00.
Send for Circulars.
The Wilder Manufacturing Co., Salem, Mass.

CLEANFONT NIPPLE

Ribbed inside, cannot stick together, cannot collapse.

SEAMLESS   RIBBED INSIDE

Sample by mail
6 cts.
50 cts. doz.
or of
ALL DRUGGISTS

FOX, FULTZ & CO.
52 Park Place, New York.   **18 Blackstone St., Boston**
Catalogue of Rubber Goods FREE

Improved Health-Lift for Physical Culture.

Given only to COMPANION subscribers for **five new subscribers**; or for **one new subscriber and $1.75 cents additional.** See Conditions, page 506. Sold for $3.50. Sent by express, charges paid by receiver. Shipping weight 30 lbs.

This is the latest and best apparatus for developing a vigorous and healthy body. Should be in every household. Adapted for children as well as adults. Many gymnasiums and schools have adopted our apparatus. The pulley-wheel hangers are made with a wide swivel motion, the handles are solid rosewood, oil polished, the drab cord is full regulation weight and size, the wall and floor blocks stained cherry. Is adapted for either 3 or 5-pound weights.

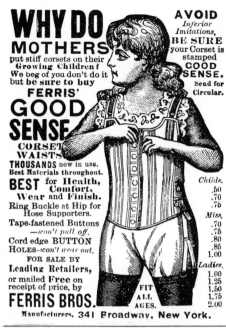

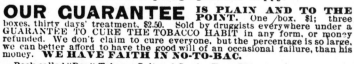

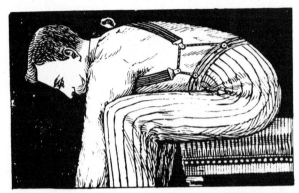

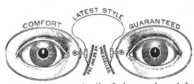

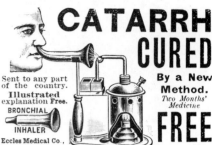

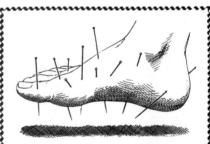

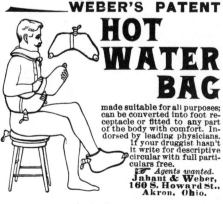

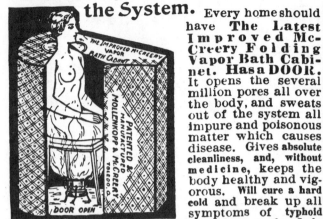
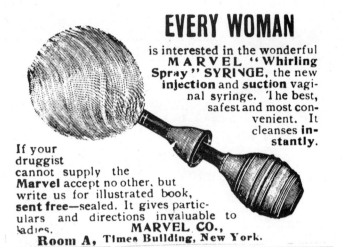

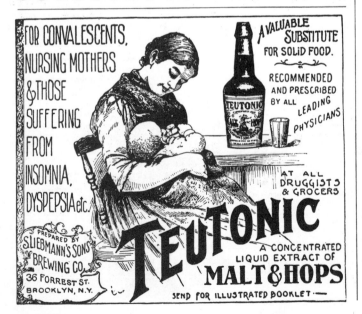

PLEASURE

COLUMBIA BICYCLE.

A practical machine for all except the old and infirm. Better than a horse, as it eats no oats; because on it you can ride more miles in a day over common roads than a horse can go. Send 3-cent stamp for price-list and 24-page catalogue, with testimonials and full information.

THE POPE MANUFACTURING CO.,
85 Summer St., Boston, Mass.

JUMP FOR JOY!!!
1776. 1876.

CRANDALL'S
CENTENNIAL JUMPING ROPE.
PATENTED, NOVEMBER 9th, 1875.

This novel invention is the only known improvement on the old jumping-rope. It must be seen to be appreciated.

With a little practice a child can become skillful in its use and find graceful movement, healthful exercise and amusement. Send for Circular.

J. A. CRANDALL, Patentee and Manufacturer, 182 Fulton Street, Brooklyn, N. Y.

PIANO-ETTES.

THE Latest Novelty PRICE, $2.50. 3,000 SOLD CHRISTMAS WEEK.

This is an entirely new article of Swiss invention, designed to take the place of a PIANO, where one can not be afforded, or to give a knowledge of Piano playing before purchasing a piano or organ. The keys and tongue are OF METAL, carefully tuned and pitched, and WILL NEVER GET OUT OF ORDER. The case is hard wood, finely finished, imitation of inlaid Mosaic. It will make a handsome ornament for any room. Any tune can readily be played upon it in less time than it takes to learn the scale on a piano. It is at once amusing, instructive, and a great help to a musical education. The music produced is soft, melodious, and very pleasing. A more appropriate present cannot be made one, and nothing will serve better to enliven the long Winter evenings. Parents, if your child has any musical taste, and you cannot afford a Piano, buy him or her a PIANO-ETTE. You will not regret it. Send by express on receipt of price. Address,

C. H. SPAULDING & CO., Importers,
95 Water St., Boston, Mass.

A complete instruction book, with twenty beautiful melodies set to music, sent to purchasers for 25 cts.

BILLIARDETTE.

We take pleasure in presenting to the public one of the most fascinating games ever introduced. It is designed for the **home,** and we believe will be welcomed everywhere.

The board being very light, it can be placed on an ordinary table; when it is not in use it can be put away in a very small space; nothing can easily get out of order, and it will be found by parents one of those much-desired attractions in the home which help to keep the children happy there.

The cut fully represents the game and the mode of playing it. The size of the board is 5 ft. 10 in. x 2 ft. 1 in.

No. 1 is very neatly gotten up, and it is an ornament for any room. There are ten balls and one cue put up with every game, together with printed instructions. Price of No. 1, **$5.00.** Expressage to be paid by the recipient.

No. 2 is of the same size as No. 1, the only difference in the two boards being that No. 2 is made of **fine Black Walnut,** the surface is covered with **extra fine Billiard Cloth,** and the balls are of

Boxwood. Price of No. 2, **$8.00.** Expressage to be paid by the recipient. Orders solicited. Rules accompany each game.

ORANGE JUDD COMPANY, Sole Agents, 245 Broadway, New York.

TRY YOUR LUCK IN LEGAL LOTTERY.

Chartered for school purposes. Drawn in public by Sworn State Commissioners on 15th and 30th of this, and every month. Bonds amounting to $200,000 given to the State to secure the payment of prizes. For tickets and circulars address

C. H. MURRAY & CO., Covington, Ky.

RUBY MAGIC LANTERN,

With Views, Lectures, Tickets, &c., for $1.50.

On receipt of 35 cents extra we will prepay express charges to any part of the United States.

PERRY MASON & CO., 41 Temple, Place, Boston, Mass.

WONDER CAMERA
THE GREATEST INVENTION OF THE AGE.

WILL SHOW ANY OPAQUE OBJECT.

Inclose stamp for Illustrated Circular.

E. I. HORSMAN, 100 William St., N. Y.,
Sole Agent for the United States.

Children's Swing. Given for one new name.

All children like to swing. It is a delightful sport. This invention makes it convenient and safe to swing in the sitting-room, parlor, kitchen, and without defacing the case of doors. It can be attached to an arbor or tree, and can be used the same in the country or city, in the summer or winter. It can be put up in a minute and more quickly removed. It is durable, safe, neat and cheap. The hooks are cast iron, held in place with springs, and covered at place of contact with rubber. Two ropes, 6 feet long, go with each outfit. Given for one new name. It must be sent by express, or will be sent by mail on receipt of 50 cts.

We offer it for sale for $1. Sent as indicated above.

THE PATENT FIELD AND LAWN TENT

FOR CROQUET AND BASE-BALL.

S. E. DROWN.

COMPOSITE IRON WORKS CO.,

MANUFACTURERS OF

Railings, Gates,

Wire Farm Fence,

Garden and Lawn Ornaments,

Vases,

Fountains, Statuary, Etc.,

109 MERCER ST.,

New York.

Young America's FAVORITE.
Bramhall, Smith & Co.,
Manufacturers,
128 Chambers St.,
New York.
Trade Supplied.

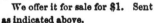

SPECIMENS DRAWN BY **THE CURVE SCRIBE.**
THE SCRIBE WILL ON COMMON COMPASSES & DRAW ANY FIGURE OR LETTERED LINE.
FULL DIRECTIONS WITH EACH INSTRUMENT.
THE HARTFORD CURVE SCRIBE CO.
294 Broadway N.Y.
Sent by mail to any order for $1.25 or with Compass $2.00.
PATENTED IN THE UNITED STATES, GREAT BRITAIN & CANADA.

Automatic Crystal Fountain.

SELF-ACTING

requiring no

Pressure of Water.

A Beautiful Holiday Gift.

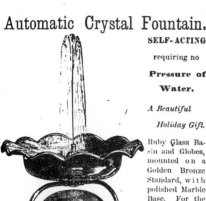

Ruby Glass Basin and Globes, mounted on a Golden Bronze Standard, with polished Marble Base. For the Parlor, Dining-room, Library, Conservatory, Store Counter, Show Window, etc. Especially adapted to purify the air in the sick-room.

The addition of Cologne to the water makes it a

PERFUME FOUNTAIN.

Height to top of basin, 21 ins.; diameter of basin, 10 ins.; height of stream 8 ins. Price complete **$15.**

Address for Descriptive Circular.

JAMES W. TUFTS,
33 to 39 Bowker St., Boston.

The Same Old, Old Story was Told Again at Three O'Clock in the Morning."

This fine large Chromo, printed in no less than *twelve colors*, with all the beauty and finish of the ten-dollar imported chromos, and in its subject one that can be felt and appreciated by all, is now offered at the unprecedentedly low rate of **20 Cents**—undoubtedly the cheapest and finest chromo ever issued for the people. The wood gives some idea of the subject, but cannot give the effect of the rich colors. For sale at all news depots and dealers who keep FRANK LESLIE'S PUBLICATIONS. Orders may be sent to

Frank Leslie, No. 537 Pearl Street, New York.

P. T. Barnum's New & Greatest Show on Earth!

My great Traveling Centennial Academy of Object Teaching cost a million and a half of dollars, employs 1,100 persons, 600 horses and ponies, and will be transported East to Maine and West to Missouri on 100 solid steel railroad cars. It by far surpasses all my former efforts; consists of sixty cages of rare wild animals and amphibia, including Barnum's $25,000 *Behemoth*, the only HIPPOPOTAMUS in America; vast Centennial Museum of living Mechanical Automata and other curiosities; a CENTENNIAL PORTRAIT GALLERY; BEST CIRCUS IN THE WORLD. A JUBILEE of Patriotic Song and Splendor; superb Historical Tableaux; National Anthems by several hundred trained voices, accompanied by music and roar of cannon; *the whole audience to rise and join in singing the national hymn, "America."* I carry my own park of Cannon and a large Church Bell, fire a national salute of 13 guns each morning, accompanied by the public bells, and give the most extensive and gorgeous STREET PAGEANT ever witnessed, glittering with patriotic features, and attended by three bands of music. Each night a grand display of Patriotic Fireworks, showing WASHINGTON, American Flags, etc., in national colors of fine red, white and blue, fine Balloons, etc. You will never see the like again. Admission to all, 50 cents. Children under nine, Half Price. P. T. BARNUM.

The Fish that comes within fooling distance never gets away!

A GRAB GAME!

Successful Fishing Reduced to a Certainty.

THE EAGLE'S CLAW !

Catches more fish, with less bait, and in less time than the most skillful fisherman can with a single hook. Catches all kinds of **Animals, Fowls, Eels, Crabs, Turtles** and all fish that bite at bait. "The best device for catching fish and game we ever saw."—OHIO FARMER. Highly recommended by the TURF, FIELD AND FARM, and the PRACTICAL FARMER. No. 1, for all ordinary fishing, the Ladies' Favorite, by mail, **35 Cents. Four for $1.00.** No. 2 for large Fish Rabbits, Foxes, Woodchucks, Minks, etc., by mail, **50 cents. Three for $1.00.** Make change with postage stamps and send bills for larger amounts. **WORLD MANUFACTURING CO.** 122 Nassau Street, New York. NOTE.—Mention this paper when you order

The Fish catch themselves by "Snap Judgement." It's real fun to watch how it gathers them in.

SUPERB DRAWING ROOM STYLES, $200 to $510 and upwards; FOR LARGE CHURCHES, $570, $480, $360 and less; FOR SMALLER CHURCHES, SCHOOLS, ETC., $84 to $200 and upwards; POPULAR STYLES in great variety, $22 to $200 and upwards. ORGANS FOR EASY PAYMENTS, $6.38 per quarter, or $5 per month and upwards. ILLUSTRATED CATALOGUES and PRICE LISTS free.

THESE ORGANS ARE CERTAINLY UNRIVALED IN EXCELLENCE, WHILE THE PRICES ARE NOT MUCH HIGHER THAN THOSE OF VERY INFERIOR INSTRUMENTS.

MASON & HAMLIN ORGAN CO.,

154 Tremont St., BOSTON ; 46 East 14th St.. (Union Square), NEW YORK ; 149 Wabash Ave., CHICAGO.

BUBBLE PARTIES.

One of the most amusing, as well as easily arranged, entertainments for the Holidays, is a "Bubble Party." Twenty or more ladies and gentlemen, enough clay pipes so each will have one, three or four bowls of soap-suds, and, say, half a dozen trifles for prizes, are all that is required, the prizes to be awarded to those who blow the largest bubbles, one of the party to act as referee.

The suds should be made of IVORY SOAP, as it gives a clean, white, and abundant lather, with an entire freedom from oil or grease ; and as the materials of which it is made are so clean and pure, it is not at all offensive to the smell or taste, like ordinary soap.

If your grocer does not keep the Ivory Soap, send six two-cent stamps to pay the postage to Procter & Gamble, Cincinnati, and they will send you *free* a large cake of IVORY SOAP.

RIEMAN & CO'S.
Photographic Parlors.

....

New Style Cabinet, Boudoir and Panel Photographs.

....

NO. 26 MONTGOMERY STREET, S. F.

TAKE THE ELEVATOR, Opp. Lick House.

This Saturday Afternoon,

Commencing at 2 o'clock P. M.,

A GRAND EXHIBITION OF SWIMMING AND DIVING

WILL TAKE PLACE AT

TERRACE BATHS, • • • • • • ALAMEDA.

UNDER THE AUSPICES OF THE

Neptune Swimming and Boating Club,
OF SAN FRANCISCO.

ORDER OF CONTESTS:

1. Race for Boys under 16 years of age,............Gold Medal
2. Race for Amateurs who have never won a prize, 2 Gold Medals
3. Plain Diving, ...2 Gold Medals
4. Race for Amateurs who have won prizes,......2 Gold Medals
5. Fancy Diving,..Gold Medal
6. Race for Professionals,.............................Cash Prize

MUSIC BY THE FIRST REGIMENT BAND.

THE WONDER OF THE AGE.

'Piano or Organ playing learned in ONE DAY!

MASON'S CHART.

A child 10 years old can understand it perfectly.

This most wonderful invention has been before the public (in its perfected form) but a short time and the sales have been immense, which is the surest test of its unparalleled merit; and orders are received from every country on the globe. It is a new theory, and a decided departure from the old method. **Mason's Chart** fits over the keys of a Piano or Organ, *indicating exactly where and how the hands are to be placed, and the proper keys to strike,* changing its position and arrangement to suit the key in which the piece is written that you wish to play. *They are perfectly infallible in their results.* If you can read you can play the Piano or Organ in **one day** *better than some teachers could teach you in three months.* If you have no Piano you can learn at some friend's house, and astonish all with your knowledge. DEXTER SMITH, the editor of the leading Musical Paper in the world, says: "*They should find a place in every house, whether there is a Piano or Organ or not. They are to Music what the Multiplication Table is to Arithmetic.*" It gives decided satisfaction in every case. It cannot do otherwise saving as it does, a hundred times its cost, and in its **great simplicity** lies its **unequalled success.** MUSIC TEACHERS THEMSELVES UNHESITATINGLY ENDORSE IT. The price is **one dollar** *for a complete set* (4 forms) and includes payment of postage by us. **$7 per doz. to Agents,** *or the trade by express.* **Special offer,** to every purchaser of MASON CHARTS who will state in what paper they saw the advertisement, and will agree to show the charts to their friends we will give as a FREE PRESENT our **Music Album** with 16 pieces of choice music, instrumental and vocal. Those wishing the Album sent by mail prepaid will enclose 10 cents extra, otherwise send by express. No one will regret learning to play the Piano or Organ, it is the greatest of all accomplishments. Address **C. H. Spaulding & Co., 57 Washington St., Boston, Mass.,** *Agents.*

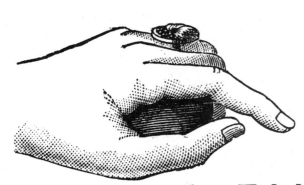

The Finger-Ring Trick.

SOMETHING NEW AND RICH.

This beautiful trick is simply (to all appearance) a fancy finger-ring, silver-plated, and being of an odd pattern, immediately arrests the attention of any friend, who will naturally ask to examine it. Attached to this ring is a small rubber ball, which is held in the palm of the hand, so as to prevent detection. This ball is filled with water, and when a person examines it that you wish to play the trick on, you have only to close your hand, which will throw a small steady stream of water directly in a person's face. Once filling the ball is sufficient to operate the trick one dozen times. If you wish to play this trick on LADIES, it may be made very agreeable by filling the ball with cologne in place of water. I will send one by mail, postage-paid, on receipt of price : 40 cts. each, or $3 per doz.; ½ doz. $1.50; for less than half-dozen, full price. If you order a sample you will send for a dozen more. Send 3-cent stamp for 24-page Illustrated Price-list of Novelties, Steam Engines, etc.

Address,

WARD B. SNYDER,
84 Fulton Street, New York City.

Our LATEST CATALOGUE of Band Instruments with 150 Engravings of Suits, Caps, Belts, Pompons, Pouches, Drum-Majors' Staffs, and Hats, Epaulets, Cap-Lamps, Stands, Outfits and Music, contains **85** pages of VALUABLE INFORMATION for MUSICIANS. Mailed free. LYON & HEALY, Monroe and State Sts., Chicago, Ill.

Active, intelligent Boys, who can count money, are making from 50 cents to $1.00 per day, after school, at home, among their playmates. Each one a complete Store, with large sign, circulars to distribute, etc., and over 450 articles of Fancy Candies, to retail at one cent each. Money doubled in a few days. "It's lots of fun." Sent by express on receipt of $2.00; full description and list of articles sent on receipt of three-cent stamp.

MITCHELL & WHITELAW,
Wholesale Confectioners, 70 Walnut St., Cincinnati, O.,
Manufacturers of all kinds of Confectionery.

A MASSIVE MOVING MIRACLE!

The Grandest and Best Circus ever in California, at San Francisco, NINE DAYS only,

............COMMENCING............

Saturday Afternoon, October 9th.

LOCATED AT CORNER OF MISSION AND SEVENTH STREETS,

REPRODUCING

—AND—

REFLECTING ALL EARTH'S GRANDEST MARVELS!

....UNDER THE....

RESPLENDENT GLARE

....OF THE....

BRUSH, DYNAMO, ELECTRIC LIGHT, USED EXCLUSIVELY

....WITH....

Circus, Menagerie, Aquarium, and Congress of Living Wonders.

Absolutely the World's Greatest Show.

FIRST APPEARANCE ON THE PACIFIC COAST OF

The World's Champion Circus Artists, FRANK A. GARDNER, surnamed the "Human Hurricane."

The Adonis of the Arena, WILLIAM O'DALE, the Only Seven-Horse Rider Living.

The Peerless Horseman, FREDERICK BARCLAY, the Greatest Character Rider on Earth.

The Greatest of All Lady Riders, MD'LLE ADELAIDE.

The Equestrian Queen, MISS FANNY MORGAN.

The Beautiful and Dashing Gymnasts, the CLAIRE SISTERS.

The Only and Original Aerial Bicycle Riders, the MESSRS. DE COMAS, Three in Number.

The Champion Acrobats of Every Clime, the FOUR LIVINGSTONS.

The Great Horizontal Bar Team, DUNBAR and RENO.

The Most Comical of All Clowns, the Laugh-Provoking "PICO."

The Great Shakesperian Jester, TOM McINTYRE.

The Great Leaping Corps, HARRY LONG, JOHN MURTZ, BURT RICHARDSON and DAN KENNEDY.

The $50,000 Troupe of Trained Stallions, whose Wonderful Feats Astound Every Beholder.

The Only Spanish Performing Bull, together with a REGIMENT OF ARTISTS AND AUXILIARIES, whose Names are Famous throughout the World, including the TWO GIANTS, CAPT. BATES AND WIFE.

650 Feet of Crawling Reptiles,   **The Mammoth Kansas Ox,**
The Baboon Family,   **A Herd of Huge Elephants,**
The Giant Mandrill Monkey and   **An Immense Menagerie,**
All Without Extra Charge.

ONE THOUSAND THRILLING NOVELTIES!

THE ELECTRIC LIGHT BURNING DAY AND NIGHT.

THE TRICK STALLIONS AT SCHOOL

Admission.............................Prices AS USUAL.

ONLY ONE TICKET

Required to all advertised Shows. 1,200 Reserved Opera Chairs, at a slight advance. Doors open at 1 o'clock and 7 o'clock P. M. Circus performances one hour later.

————o————

A Grand Illuminated MARDI-GRAS Street Parade will be given FRIDAY NIGHT, OCTOBER 8TH.

This glittering Pagent will start from the Amphitheatre at 7 o'clock, and traverse all principal streets.

THE EMPRESS OF THE ARENA

A PICTURE THAT TELLS ITS OWN STORY.

Scroll-Sawing ought to be encouraged in every home where there are boys and girls. It cultivates a love for *beautifying* the home; it developes a *mechanical* taste and it keeps boys at home *pleasantly* and usefully employed, who might otherwise be running in the streets. This cut shows how easily Scroll Sawing is done. The beautiful articles on the table speak for themselves.

Our *Improved Bracket Saw Frame* is now made from the best spring steel, has a solid rosewood handle, and is beautifully nickel-plated. With it you can make Brackets, Clocks, Picture Frames, Easels, Fancy Articles, etc., of the most exquisite beauty. With only 40 cents worth of wood you can make articles worth from $1 to $3 each.

This outfit now consists of 1 Nickel-Plated Bracket Saw, 5x12 inches; 12 Extra Saw Blades; 1 Manual Sawing and Wood Carving; 100 Miniature Designs; Designs for $25 worth of Brackets, etc., etc., full size; 1 Drill Point. Price, complete, only $1.00; postage and packing, 20 cents.

For several years it has been a study with us to furnish our subscribers the means for *Practical Home Industries.* We originated our popular Scroll Saw Outfit in 1874. At that time there was nothing of the kind in the United States excepting some heavy German Saw Frames, costing $8.00 each, and a few costly imported designs.

Through our efforts our subscribers can now obtain for only **$1.00** a better outfit than could have been obtained in 1874 for $6.50.

As an extra inducement for our subscribers to become interested in this beautiful work, we make this offer: To all persons ordering this outfit we will give free **3 dozen extra Saw Blades.** The offer will be good only to April 1, 1883.

PERRY MASON & CO., 41 Temple Place, Boston, Mass.

Publishers Youth's Companion.

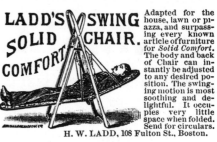

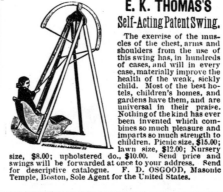

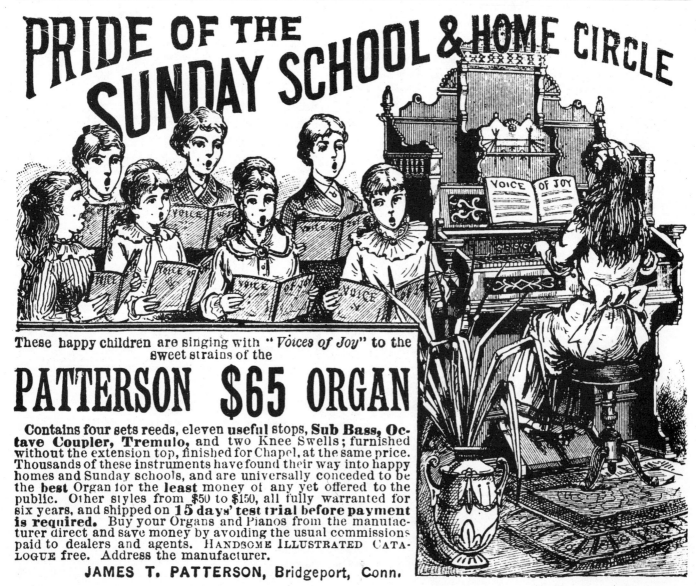

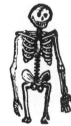
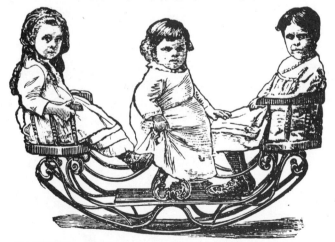

CHRISTMAS MORNING.
"Oh Papa and Mamma! How good of you! And you have remembered the **Lundborg** Perfumes and Cologne that I asked you for, too! Oh! Oh! Oh!"

Solar Printing Outfit. Given for one new name.

This consists of a regular photographer's printing frame, nicely padded, with a hinged back. With it we give sixteen sheets of chemically prepared paper, 5x8 inches in size. Let

a *photographer* make you a *negative* of your own picture, and you can print as many photographs from it as you wish. With the outfit you can make beautiful pictures of ferns, leaves, copies of small engravings, &c. The sun does the work, as you see in the cut. No chemicals are used. We also give with it glass negatives for 10 beautiful pictures from Doré's Bible Gallery. You can photograph hundreds of beautiful pictures with these negatives. Given for one new name. Price, $1. **Postage and packing, 18 cts.**, when sent as a premium or purchased.

Full instructions, etc., etc., all packed in a sliding cover wooden box. The Press is a perfect Printing Press in every respect, and will print Cards, Labels, Tags, etc., as well as high-cost machines. The press is made entirely of malleable iron, with wrought-iron rivets and steel screws, and is japanned and ornamented. Size of Box 10x4½ inches, and 3½ inches wide.

THIS SPECIAL AND GREAT OFFER sent to any address on receipt of

!!! ONLY $1.50 !!!

The express charges, which are very small, can be paid on receipt of the press.

PERRY MASON & CO.

SOMETHING NEW.

The LIGHTNING DART WHEEL, the pet game of the day, Patented May 12th, 1874.

This beautiful and interesting game, which has recently been introduced, has established its reputation beyond a doubt by its rapid sale during the holidays. No list of household games complete without it. For sale by Toy and Game dealers. Also sent by mail enclosed in a neat box, postage paid, on receipt of its reduced price, 75 cts.
Address, **LANE BROTHERS & CO.,**
East Swanzey, N. H.

THE BRADLEY TWO-WHEELER

Send for Free Circular "How to purchase direct from the manufacturer." Address
Absolutely free from Horse Motion. **SYRACUSE, N. Y.**
BRADLEY & CO. 22 COLLEGE PLACE, NEW YORK.
32 S. MARKET ST., BOSTON.

Mothers and Babies Made Happy!

By using STEIN-BACH'S New Patent Adjustable COACH, COUCH and CRADLE! with PAVILION TOP, Telescoping Handle, New and Safe WHEEL-LOCKING DEVICE, REVERSIBLE HAIR CUSHION, and other decided Improvements.
SALUTARY REFORM in BABY COACHES!
SEAT INSTANTLY TRANSFORMED into a BED!
BABY RAISING MADE EASY!
INFANTS NOT TORTURED WHEN FALLEN ASLEEP WHILE SEATED!
NOT OVERHEATED ON FEATHER BEDS!
Never DISTURBED in their SLUMBER!
PROTECTION against ALL CONTINGENCIES!
Every Coach WARRANTED for ONE YEAR!
BEST MATERIAL and WORKMANSHIP!
None SUPERIOR! None more PRACTICAL!
Can be used TWELVE months in the YEAR!
For Illustrated List, address
GEO. P. STEINBACH,
Patentee and Manufacturer. Baltimore. Md.

The White Mountain Hammock Chair.

The White Mountain Hammock Chair

Differs from all other stationary or reclining chairs, in that it is better, simpler, and cheaper. It is far superior to a Hammock in every way, and can be put up so as to be always in the shade.

It assumes and can be used in any position, from sitting up to lying down, without any exertion of the occupant, and supports and rests the body in whatever position it is placed.

The foot-rest can be quickly and easily adjusted to suit the tallest or shortest persons. The seat is made of strong canvas, fitting perfectly the entire length without drawing the clothing tightly around the body, thus making it as cool as a Hammock, while the annoyance of catching buttons, tearing down the hair, &c., is avoided.

It is adapted to the house, lawn, porch or camp, weighs only twelve pounds and occupies only four inches in thickness, when folded, and is pronounced by every one, "the best article in the world for the enjoyment of fresh air," while the price is within the reach of all.

For the convenience of those who have no piazza or trees from which to suspend the chair, we have lately invented and are now manufacturing a wooden frame which can be instantly taken apart and folded in a light package only 3 inches square.

Price of Chair, . $4.00 each.
Price of Frame, . $1.00 each.

—

GOODELL COMPANY,

ANTRIM, N. H.,

Sole Manufacturers.

An *ILLUSTRATED CATALOGUE of MAGIC LANTERNS and STEREOPTICONS*, for Public, Sunday-school, and Home Exhibitions, 124 pages, will be sent FREE to any address; also a copy of "The Exhibitor," a Quarterly Magazine, devoted to the interests of those who use the MAGIC LANTERN for instruction, amusement, or profit. Address

C. T. MILLIGAN, 728 Chestnut Street, Philadelphia,

ANOTHER GENERATION

OF BOYS AND GIRLS has come to the front since we first popularized the beautiful art of Fret-Sawing in America. Every boy and every girl of this new generation ought to own one of our splendid Nickel Plated

Fret Saws, 5x12 inches, with Rose-wood Handle. With each Saw we give Impression Paper; 1 Manual of Sawing and Wood Carving; Full-sized Designs for $25 worth of Brackets, etc.; 1 Drill, and Extra Blades.

WITH OUR BRACKET SAW OUTFIT tens of thousands of homes have been made more beautiful, young people have made money, money has been earned, and time (often spent in the streets) has been usefully and profitably employed. For a better description of this Outfit, see our PREMIUM LIST, page 434. The Outfit sent to any address complete, *postage paid by us,* for $1.25.
PERRY MASON & CO., 41 Temple Place, Boston, Mass.

PAPER FLOWER OUTFIT.
Only First Quality Materials used in this Outfit.
THIS OFFER GOOD FOR 6 MONTHS. INSTRUCTION BOOK, 6 CTS.

The latest and a most important development of the use of Tissue paper is the imitation of flowers. Very much can be done in the way of decoration by the use of simple means. In the past a mistaken idea prevailed that the beauty of a thing depended upon costly material and elaborate workmanship, so decoration was left to a few skilled hands, and was only possible to the wealthy. There is no reason why every home should not be beautified with flowers and the innumerable little things that can be easily and quickly made from the Tissue paper now imported. The perfection of this Outfit is the result of long experience and careful labor on the part of the manufacturers. *Outfits sent Post-paid.*

OUR $1.00 OUTFIT contains 24 sheets best French Tissue paper, assorted colors, 1 doz. Sprays, Wire, Rubber Stemming, Flower Centers, Stamped Flowers, Culots, Leaves, Moss, Pincers, Daisy Petals, and Book of Instructions.

BEGINNERS' OUTFIT, 35 CTS. Contains Tissue, Wire, Leaves, Culots, Tubing for Stems, Sprays, and Book of Instructions. Address

ART MFG. CO., Deep River, Conn.

"DRINK FAIR, BETSEY, WOTEVER YOU DO."
Martin Chuzzlewit.

TEA CLUB ORDERS.

We have made a specialty for six years of *giving away* as Premiums, to those who get up clubs for our goods, *Dinner and Tea Sets, Gold Band Sets, Silverware, etc.* Teas of all kinds, from 30 to 75 cents per pound. We do a very large Tea and Coffee business, besides sending out from 60 to 90 **CLUB ORDERS** each day. **SILVER-PLATED CASTERS** as Premiums with **$5, $7** and **$10** orders. **WHITE TEA SETS** with **$10** orders. **DECORATED TEA SETS** with **$15. GOLD BAND** or **MOSS ROSE SETS** of **44 pieces**, or **DINNER SETS of 106 pieces**, with **$20** orders, and a **Host** of other Premiums. Send us postal and mention this paper, and we will send you full **Price and Premium List.** Freight charges average 75 cents per 100 pounds to points West.

GREAT LONDON TEA CO.,
801 Washington Street, Boston, Mass.

FOR VACATION DAYS.

The Raymond Patent Extension Speed Skate.

A pair given for one new name, and 25 cts. additional.

Skating.

Last season's skating was a failure in many localities. Warm weather and no ice are not favorable to the king of winter sports. We trust that Jack Frost will, this coming winter, prove himself more friendly to the army of young people who are anxiously waiting his approach.

Last year we first introduced the Raymond Extension Speed Skates. They have proved to be the most satisfactory Skates we have offered. As a Speed Skate they are remarkable.

Noted for Strength.

From several thousand pairs we sent out not a single pair was broken. For strength, speed, and beauty of finish these Skates are all that can be desired. Three years ago they sold for $2.50 per pair.

Boys' feet will grow. So will Raymond's Extension Speed Skates.

We will explain. Suppose George, at nine years of age, buys any of the old-style Skates. At twelve years he has outgrown them, and must obtain a larger pair. Not so with the **Raymond Extension.** As the boy's feet grow he lets out a notch in the Extension Foot-Plate. Thus, year by year, while growing, his Skates can be adjusted to fit. He will thus be saved the cost of buying a larger pair.

As these Skates are so strong they will out-wear the average boy's skating years.

Strong and Well Made.

These are the best finished Skates for the price we have ever offered to our subscribers. They are warranted against any imperfection in manufacture. When you order the Skates, send us the size in inches, according to the following table, and we will send them to you already adjusted to fit your boot.

How to Order.

Measure the sole of your boot from extreme end of heel to extreme end of toe, and send us the length in inches, as below, adding postage, according to the size of the Skate you order, as indicated. Boys clubbing together, and ordering Skates sent by express to one address, can save about one-half the expressage.

SIZE IN INCHES.	POSTAGE AND PACKING.
8	50 cts.
8½	50 "
9	50 "
9½	50 "
10	50 "
10½	50 "
11	55 "
11½	55 "

A pair given for one new name, and 25 cts. additional. Our price, only $1.25 per pair. If you wish them sent by mail, you must add the postage as indicated above, or they can be sent by express, and charges paid by receiver, which in many cases will be much cheaper.

A GIFT WORTH HAVING.

(Feminine Chorus): Oh! isn't it lovely! I must have a Kodak!

Send to The Eastman Company, Rochester, N.Y. for a copy of "Do I want a Camera," (illustrated) free by mail.

KIMBALL BROS.,

Kensingtons, Reversible seats,
Irvington Wagons, four passenger,
Manhattan Cabriolets, Extension and Canopy,
Beach Wagons Painted and Natural Woods,
Albert Phaetons, open or Victoria top, C-spring,
Loupe Park Phaetons for Ladies Calling and Shopping,
Ladies' Duquesitas, with or without Rumble,
Buckboards, two, four and six passenger, Antique Woods,
Rockaways with Childs' seat, and Octagon with Drop seat,
Octagon Broughams, Broughams, Coupes, Landaus and Berlins,
Special Traps built to order, estimates and drawings furnished.

Factory and Warerooms, 110, 112 & 114 Sudbury St., Boston.

"OUR DONKEY PARTY."—A world of fun and indescribable laughter—Putting the Tail on the Donkey. Donkey party consists of a donkey-sheet and 12 tails. Putting the tail in its proper place is no easy matter, and affords much amusement to all present. Prizes can be given same as in progressive euchre. Sample sent by mail pre-paid on receipt of 50 cts. A liberal discount to the trade. Agents wanted. E. I. HORSMAN, 80 & 82 William St., N.Y.

GOAT HARNESS
From $1.50 to $12.50 a Set.

GOAT CARTS $4.00 TO $7.00

Write for illustrated catalogue and prices of GOAT HARNESS and GOAT CARTS. Address
FRANK B. BARKLEY MFG. CO.,
271 and 273 Main Street, CINCINNATI, O.

Improved Mechanical Telephone.

Given for one new name.

The practical value of Telephones has become so well known that their use is becoming very general. For lines up to one thousand feet this instrument is especially adapted. The speaking powers are loud and distinct.

A good business can be done by putting up these Telephones for customers. You can either sell the instrument or charge a fair price per month for its use. Many boys are now doing this.

What the Telephone Outfit contains. Two Perfection Transmitters—one for each end of the line; Leather Cords and Loops, and Supports for putting up the Wire, and three hundred feet of Wire. Full instructions.

Given for one new name. Price, $1. **Postage and packing, 25 cts.,** when sent as a premium or purchased. Additional Wire furnished at 30 cts. per 100 feet, postage paid by us.

"The Companion" Tennis Racquet, Nets

and Balls. Companion Racquet given for one new name, and $1 additional. 12-Thread Net, 36 feet by 3 feet, given for one new name, and 50 cts. additional. Wright & Ditson Tennis Balls, two given for one new name, and 10 cts. additional.

Lawn Tennis has now become a National Summer Out-door Game. Our Companion Tennis Racquet is made especially for us, and is a first-class article, full size, carefully bent, well strung with good gut in fine meshes, 25 by 18 strands, hard red-wood seared handle. Such a Racquet usually sells for $5. We shall sell this one this year for only $2.75. Premium offer above. **Postage and packing, 25 cts.,** when sent as a premium or purchased.

This delightful game [Patented] complete for 4 tables, 16 persons; including 80 Brass Fish, Brass and Nickel Poles and Hooks, Gold and Silver Lines, Gold and Silver Markers, Score Cards for each player, Rules in French and English, Pools of Coppered Wire. All in a handsome case covered in imitation alligator, price, $5.00. (Extra tables, $1.25 each) Special holiday sets of finest Parisian workmanship for four tables, $10.00; five tables, $12.50. If your dealer hasn't it, address,

THE PROGRESSIVE ANGLING COMPANY, 465 Broad Street, Newark, N. J.

PROGRESSIVE ANGLING.

"SOCIETY'S LATEST FAD."

"Do you Angle?" That is a question of paramount imortance in society at present; if you do not "Angle" you had better learn how as soon as you can, for "Angling" is destined to take the place of progressive euchre. In fact, the game bears a striking resemblance to that once popular social pastime. As now played in society it is progressive, and that is one feature in which the two games resemble each other; then there are prizes for the most successful player, and that constitutes another. . . . It is simple and unique. Society always likes to have something new and not very difficult of comprehension to cudgel its brains over. If not a novelty it is "too old, you know," and if not simple enough "a deuced bore."—*From Society article in Chicago Tribune.*

"Progressive Angling:" fun without stint and innocent as A B C.—*Wanamaker's Philadelphia Advertisement.*

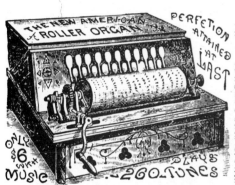

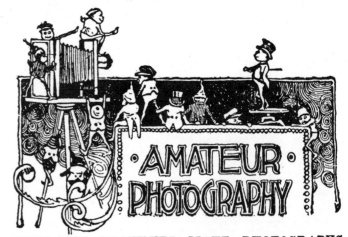

The Little Store Keeper's Outfit, with Cash Carrier.

Given for one new name.

Our Latest for Young People.

This is one of our most attractive premiums for the young people. It consists of, 1st, A Box containing an assortment of Toy Money, representing gold and silver coin to the amount of $100. 2d, Four sheets of Labels, 140 in all, to be cut up and attached separately to packages of bran or sawdust, supposed to contain whatever is printed on the Label. 3d, A form for making Paper Bags, with an assortment of bag paper. 4th, A printed price list of general merchandise, groceries, dry goods, fancy goods, hardware, etc., etc. 5th, One Rapid Transit Cash Carrier. The Cash Carrier is complete, ready to set up, as seen in the cut. A bright boy and girl will need no instruction as to the proper way to "run a store."

Not only will this novel premium serve to amuse and entertain, but it will teach the children in a very practical way the use of money, how to make change rapidly, how to buy and sell, and to transact business.

Given for one new name. Price, $1.25. Postage and packing, 25 cts., when sent as a premium or purchased. This will prove a popular game.

The Fire Engine, "Neptune." Given for only one new name.

The Engine is 14 inches long, mounted upon wheels, double-acting Force Pump, brass cylinders, air chamber, and a 12-inch rubber hose, will throw a small stream of water 25 feet. This Toy will appeal to the hearts of all bright little boys.

Given for one new name. Price, $1. Sent by express, and charges paid by receiver, when sent as a premium or purchased. The cut of the Engine, for lack of room, is not shown.

Lawn and Parlor Ring Toss. Given for one new name.

This consists of a chestnut Box containing five Hoops and a pointed and ornamented Post, on to which they can be thrown. It is a popular Game. Given for one new name. Price, 85 cts. Postage and packing, 40 cts., when sent as a premium or purchased. The cut is not shown.

200,000 Elegant Family Portraits
IN AMERICAN HOMES.

The Best Agency Business in the World.

We furnish *good agents* anywhere in the U. S. Horse and Wagon outfits, like cut, on very liberal conditions. Write for particulars and send stamp. *No postal cards noticed.* TEN EYCK PORTRAIT CO., Auburn, N. Y.

NEW PARLOR GAME.

Patented Feb. 19, 1889-90.

The whole world are being made happy with this Intensely Amusing Game. Mailed post-paid until Christmas.

Post-paid,
Nickel, $1
Bronze .75

ELASTIC TIP CO., Corner Cornhill & Wash. Sts., Boston, Mass., U. S. A.

Also Patentees of RUBBER ELASTIC FURNITURE TIPS.

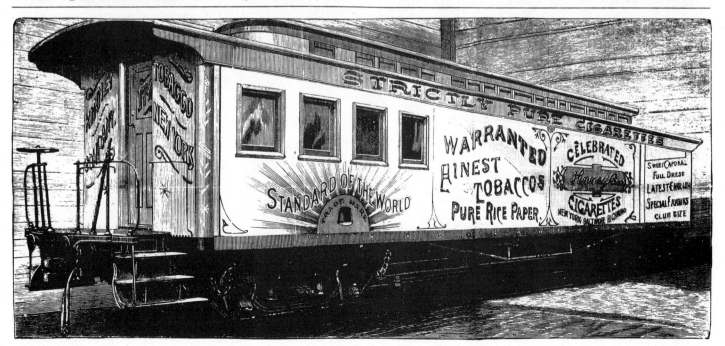

The White Eagle Skate Sail.

Given for one new name, and 35 cts. additional.

This Sail consists of more than thirty square feet of strong cotton cloth stretched upon a Frame. This Frame is formed of a tough ash mast and spars, which are held together by cast metal sockets.

The Frame can be easily put together and separated, and the Sail as easily attached to and removed from the Frame. When folded, the Sail and Frame make a light roll four feet long and two or three inches thick.

This beautiful Skate Sail given for one new name, and 35 cts. additional. Price, $1.50 each. It must be sent by express, and charges paid by receiver, when sent as a premium or purchased.

Special Offer. On receipt of only $2.50 we will send 1 Skate Sail and 1 pair of Raymond Extension Skates.

"Aw—! Mrs. Goodtaste, what did you say was the name of that jolly scent for the handkerchief you had on the steamer last Fall, and where can I buy it?"

"You mean Lundborg's EDENIA. It is manufactured down town, here in New York, but you can get it at almost any drug or fancy goods store."

LUNDBORG'S PERFUME.

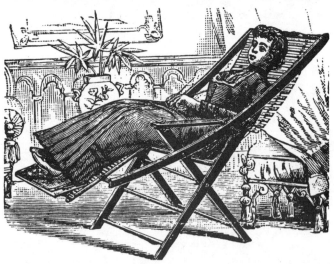

VAN HOUTEN'S COCOA

best &goes farthest.

Flimsy, inaccurate, badly printed and generally cheap looking cards detract from surroundings however handsome, and offend fastidious players. "Capitol," "Sportsman's," "Cabinet," "Army and Navy," "Treasury," and "Congress" brands of cards are not only elegant, but also acceptable to experienced players.   Insist upon having them from your dealer.

"The Card Player's Companion," showing how games are played, and giving prices of 40 brands, 400 kinds, of playing cards, will be sent to any one who will mention where this advertisement was seen and enclose a two-cent stamp.

THE U. S. PRINTING CO., RUSSELL & MORGAN FACTORIES, CINCINNATI, O.

This trade-mark is the Ace of Spades card and is on every pack and cover of the genuine. Look for it.

CRAB APPLE BLOSSOM

TRADE-MARK Reg'd

THE **NEW PERFUME** OF THE **CROWN PERFUMERY CO.** 177 NEW BOND ST. LONDON.

SOLD EVERYWHERE.

JOINTED
Cloth Doll.

Patented.

This Doll, 14 inches in length, is printed in lifelike colors on cloth with lines showing where to cut out and sew together.   It is to be stuffed with cotton or bran, and is jointed in the arms and legs so it can be made to sit in a chair or appear in any natural position.

See Illustration.

Price on one-half yard of cloth,

10 cents.
For Sale by Your Dealer.

If he has not got them show him this advertisement and he will get it for you.

Do not send to us as we have none at retail.

See full page in COMPANION PREMIUM LIST for "Tabby Cat," "Pug Dog," "Skye Terrier," "Rabbit," "Monkey," "Owl," "Little Red Riding Hood," and "Negro Dollie."

Arnold Print Works,
NORTH ADAMS, MASS.

ADORN YOUR HOME

with our artistic **Diaphanies**
(Colored Transparent Glass Pictures).

Most magnificent decoration for Windows, Transoms, Skylights, Door Panels of Hotels, Churches, Private Residences, and all places where Art Glass is used.

WELL ASSORTED STOCK OF ALL KINDS OF PICTURES.

Unparalleled as Holiday and Wedding Presents.

Our Illustrated Catalogue, containing about 600 Illustrations, will be mailed on receipt of 25 cents. Colored Catalogue, $1.00. Amount refunded in case of $10.00 order.

GRIMME & HEMPEL, 310 Broadway, New York.

Main House and Factory, Leipzig, Germany.

Just the Thing for a Holiday Present.

DAESTU

THE WONDROUS WRITING POWER

"DAESTU" commends itself to intelligent and scientific minds and is destined to electrify the civilized world.

It is the ultimate development and perfection of other devices, having for their object the demonstration of the theory that thought can be transmitted by means of an involuntary medium.

"DAESTU" conclusively demonstrates this, as by its means the mind of one person can cause the hand of another to involuntarily write the answer to a question asked mentally.

For sale by dealers in Holiday Goods,
Or by mail free on receipt of $1.50.

E. I. HORSMAN, Manufacturer, 341 Broadway, New York.

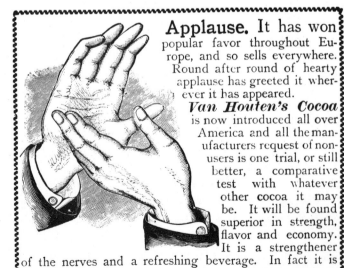

"ONE WHOLE DAY SAVED."

The traveler on the

Chicago, Rock Island and Pacific Railroad's

Special Vestibuled Fast Train, popularly known as "The Big Five," saves a whole day in the trip between Chicago and Denver. It makes close connection with the trunk lines from the East, and is a luxurious train throughout. Parlor, Dining, Buffet, Library, Smoking and Sleeping Cars are included in its equipment. A corresponding train leaves Denver every day.

The "Big Five" leaves Chicago at 10 P.M., one hour after arrival of Eastern trains, arriving at Omaha next day at noon, Denver 7.40 in the morning—the traveler being out but one day and two nights, instead of two days and one night. The next time you are going West try the "Big Five."

E. ST. JOHN, *General Manager.*
W. I. ALLEN, - *Assistant General Manager.*
JNO. SEBASTIAN, *Gen. Ticket and Pass'r Agent.*

UNRIVALLED FOR SWEETNESS AND SYMPATHY OF TOUCH.

Ivers & Pond Pianos.
Catalogue free.
Ivers & Pond Piano Co.
183 Tremont Street,
Boston, Mass.

CUSTARD WITHOUT EGGS!

CRESCENT BICYCLES "SKY HIGH"

WESTERN WHEEL WORKS. BUILDERS CHICAGO NEW YORK SEND FOR CATALOGUE

'NEATH CHILL DECEMBER'S BLAST, SWEET SUMMER BLOOMS AGAIN IN

THE MATCHLESS PERFUME MURRAY & LANMAN'S FLORIDA WATER FOR HANDKERCHIEF, TOILET, AND BATH.

AN IDEAL CHRISTMAS GIFT.

Emerson Boomerang Target Gun.

The Most Astonishing Target Gun ever Invented.

Will throw a Boomerang Arrow nearly a hundred feet, and then cause it to **return** to a **Target** at the sender's side. A seeming impossibility and yet true. Men, women and children are equally fascinated.

The Emerson Boomerang Target Gun is now the great attraction for the lawn and field. In hot weather no better game can be desired. Running and excessive exertion not necessary. Only think of it! Your Boomerang Arrows return to the Target at your side!

The Emerson Boomerang Target Gun given only to COMPANION subscribers for **one new** subscriber and **25 cents** for postage. See Premium Conditions on page 530 of our October Premium List. Sold for 80 cts., postage 25 cts. extra.

Publishers The Youth's Companion, 201 Columbus Avenue.   **PERRY MASON & CO., Boston, Mass.**

CHEESE FANCIERS

everywhere find a pleasing Delicacy in the soft, rich

American Club House Cheese.

"It Tickles the Palate."

It's Worthy a Place on the Best Tables. Put up in hermetically sealed glass jars. A miniature jar of the Cheese will be sent to any address on receipt of 10c. in stamps. "**I am exceedingly pleased with the Cheese.**"—Mrs. S. T. Rorer.

Chandler & Rudd Co., 36 Euclid Ave., Cleveland, O.

PRIMLEY'S CALIFORNIA FRUIT CHEWING GUM.

Sweetens the Breath, Aids Digestion and Prevents Dyspepsia. No other like it. **SOLD EVERYWHERE. INSIST ON PRIMLEY'S.**

FREE BOOKS TO GUM BUYERS.
Send five outside wrappers of either California Fruit or Primley's Pepsin Chewing Gum and 10 cents, and we will send you Beatrice Harraden's famous book, "Ships That Pass in the Night." List of 1700 fine books sent free on application.

"America Photographed," in 20 parts; each part contains 16 beautiful pictures, 11 x 13 inches. Any single part sent for one wrapper and six cents.

J. P. PRIMLEY,
CHICAGO, ILLS.

THE SWEETEST THING ON EARTH

If You Want Heaps of Fun

BY MAIL $1.00 POSTPAID

BUY THE Harmless Rubber-Tipped Arrow Game.

Just the thing for amusement these long winter evenings. Best parlor game ever invented. Popular throughout the civilized world. Over 2,000,000 sold. **Makes a Splendid Gift.**

If your dealer hasn't it, send us mail order. Game complete—Harmless Pistol, Target and Three Rubber-Tipped Arrows, sent post-paid for $1.00.

ELASTIC TIP CO., 370 Atlantic Ave., BOSTON, MASS.
115 Lake St., Chicago.   735 Market St., San Francisco.

Agents Wanted.

Bailey's Swimming Glove.

LIKE A DUCK'S FOOT.

Learn to swim, to float, to become in water as expert as a **DUCK** by using Bailey's Rubber Swimming Glove. They are made of Pure Para Rubber, which makes a web between the fingers like a duck's foot, doubling the power of the stroke, and greatly increasing the speed, ease, and pleasure of swimming.

Men's, $2; Women's, $1.75; Children's, $1.50 Pair.

Sent postage paid on receipt of price.

C. J. BAILEY & CO.,
Everything in Rubber Goods.
22 Boylston St., Boston.

Pat. applied for

MAGIC TOY and SUN SPECTACLES.

(Patent Applied For.)

Our attention has been called to this novelty, which is sure to be a popular one. It is brought out by the Hartford Paper Goods Co. of Hartford, Conn., and is both amusing and useful.

As TOY SPECTACLES they provoke "loads of fun." Many laughable changes in expression may be produced by turning the eye-disks to different angles. A small aperture in each disk-centre enables the wearer to see through readily.

As SUN SPECTACLES they are worn reversed, showing only the plain sides of the disks. They thus serve as useful protectors for the eyes against the glare of sun and snow, as the apertures admit only enough light for comfort.

These spectacles retail for **TEN CENTS EACH,** and will be sent postpaid on receipt of price. A liberal discount is offered to the trade.

IF YOU ARE A PIPE SMOKER

WE WANT YOU TO TRY

GOLDEN SCEPTRE

SMOKING TOBACCO.

All the talk in the world will not convince you so quickly as a trial that it is almost **PERFECTION.** We will send on receipt of 10c. a sample to any address. Prices of Golden Sceptre, 1 lb., $1.30; ¼ lb., 40 cents, postage paid. Catalogue free.

SURBRUG, 159 Fulton St., N. Y. City.

Yale MIXTURE
A Gentleman's Smoke

Does Your Saddle Hurt?

THEN RIDE

THE DUPLEX SAFETY SADDLE

SEE THAT SPRING!

Above Poster, 14x21 inches, 3 colors, postpaid, 10c.

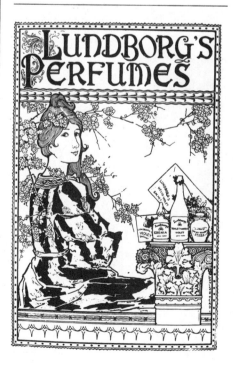

LUNDBORG'S PERFUMES

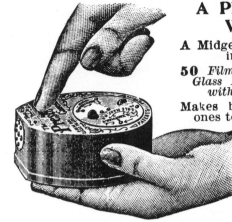

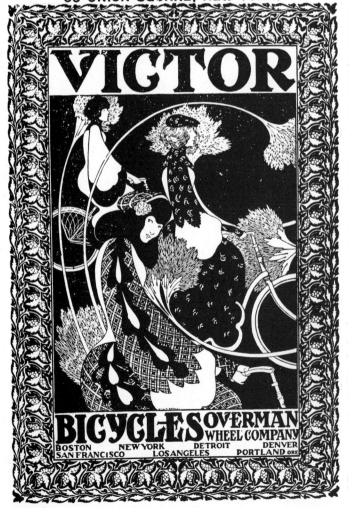

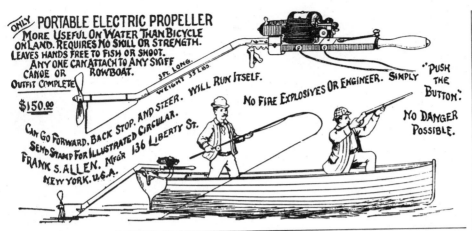

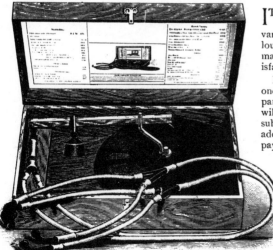

70/1896

Built for Two!

When baby number two arrives and number one has to give up the carriage to the newcomer and either walk or be dumped in, in front—there's trouble. If he walks he gets tired and cross. If he rides in front there's no comfort for either one and they both get cross! You need a carriage with our patent

Dickey Seat,

where the eldest child can ride happy, secure, and proud as a coachman. When not in use it is moved close up to back of carriage basket and makes a most convenient parcel-carrier. Before you buy a carriage by all means see ours with the patent Dickey Seat.

If you have a good carriage we'll sell you the seat alone, and any carpenter will quickly attach it for you.

...ASK AT YOUR DEALERS...

to see the **Dann** carriage with the Dickey Seat. Send name on postal for our catalogue of baby carriages and go-carts, or separate catalogue of invalids' wheel-chairs.

RATTAN MFG. COMPANY, New Haven, Conn.

MISCELLANEOUS

Blake's One Dollar Patent Chair Spring.

AGENTS WANTED. Can make $25 per day. Price reduced to Agents. The only place to purchase of the sole proprietor and manufacturer. Send for circular. GEO. K. GOODWIN, 612 Broadway.

Lower the top to an angle of 45 degrees,

Shut one eye and read at your ease.

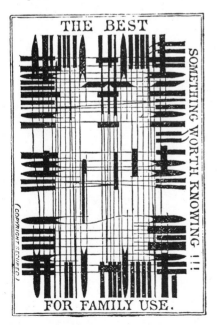

THE BEST

SOMETHING WORTH KNOWING !!!

(COPYRIGHT SECURED.)

FOR FAMILY USE.

505 BROADWAY, New York.

THE GREATEST NOVELTY OF THE AGE.

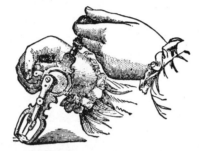

THE POCKET SEWING MACHINE,

Specially adapted for Quilting, Embroidering and Braiding.

Easily used—being held in the hand, and traverses the material to be quilted or embroidered; works with great rapidity, and gives entire satisfaction. Follows any design stamped on the cloth. Sent by mail, to any part of the United States. Plain Steel Machine, $5; Heavy Silver Plated Machine, $8. State Rights for sale. Address A. S. GILCHRIST, Secretary Pocket Sewing Machine Company, 17 Wall street, New York. tf

---

EAGLE GAS HEATING STOVES,

POSITIVELY GUARANTEED TO BE FREE FROM **SMOKE** OR **SMELL.**

WILL HEAT Offices, Parlor, Dining, Sleeping and Bath Rooms.

SEND FOR DESCRIPTIVE CATALOGUE.

Eagle Gas Stove Manufacturing Company,

636 BROADWAY,

NEW YORK.

TURNER'S PATENT LADDER

FRUIT OR STEP LADDER   FRUIT OR SELF-SUPPORTING

Is Readily Lengthened or Shortened, Self-Supporting, Easily Transported, Convertible into a Step-Ladder or Scaffold.

IT IS USEFUL TO

FARMERS, FRUIT GROWERS,

MECHANICS AND HOUSEKEEPERS.

Single Ladders forwarded, freight prepaid to nearest Station, on receipt of retail price.

AGENTS WANTED in every County.

For Circular and terms, address

Turner's Patent Extension Ladder,

P. O. Box 2,018, or No. 128 S. Front st.,
659-61cow   PHILADELPHIA.

BRASS & ZINC

STAIR PLATES

FOR

HOTELS

Public Buildings,

AND

Tenement Houses.

W. T. & J. Mersereau,

62 Duane St., N. Y.

Manufacturers of

STAIR-RODS.

1865–1870/75

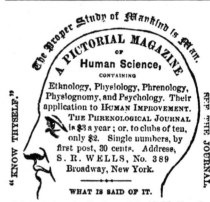

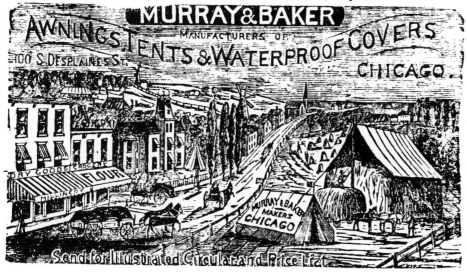
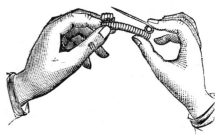

FRED. J. MILLER,
BUILDER OF
Hook & Ladder Trucks,
HOSE CARRIAGES ETC.,
AND MANUFACTURER OF
Fire Department Supplies
OF EVERY DESCRIPTION.

☞ Send for Complete Illustrated Price List.

GOODELL'S
WHITE MOUNTAIN POTATO PARER.

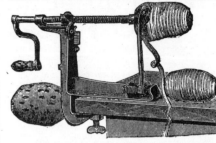

The White Mountain Potato Parer is the only machine ever made that will not only pare a potato much better than it can be done by hand, taking off a thinner paring from every shape or kind of Potato, but will go into and clean out the eyes, and altogether at a saving of at least **twenty per cent.** It is free from the objections made to the old style of rattle-trap, geared parers; is solid and substantial, cannot get out of order, and so cheap as to be within the means of everybody. Almost any of the Potato Parers in the market seem as if they might do the work better "next time," but the "White Mountain" does it now. *Every machine warranted as represented.* Ask your hardware merchant for them. Price **$1.00,** by mail, prepaid. **GOODELL CO.,**
Sole Manufacturers, Antrim, N. H.

THE
ARGAND BASE-BURNER.

Seven sizes without ovens. Six sizes with high ovens. Two sizes with low ovens. Three sizes of Parlor Heaters. The original of this class! All others in the market are copies and infringements.

PERRY & CO.,
Albany; Chicago, Ill.; New York City.

FAC SIMILE OF WORK PERFORMED BY THEM

They work wonders in a family, and are indispensable to every lady desirous of making up elegant wearing apparel.

No Sewing Machine complete without one.

LADIES, ASK YOUR SEWING MACHINE
AGENTS TO SEE THEM.

———

C. W. HANDY & CO., Sole Agents.
330 BROADWAY, N. Y

REFRIGERATOR.
JOEL TIFFANY,   CHAS. F PIERCE,
Patentee.   Manager.

TIFFANY
REFRIGERATOR
CAR COMPANY,
FOR TRANSPORTATION OF
BEEF, POULTRY, EGGS, BUTTER, FRUIT,
and all kinds of perishable goods, summer and winter.
74 Washington Street, Chicago, Ill.
Send for Circular of Trial Trips.

GREATER IMPROVEMENTS IN
Fireplace Heaters and Wrought-iron
FURNACES.
See this New Heater and our **New Metropolitan Wrought-iron Furnace** before you purchase. We guarantee greater Heating Power, Durability, and Economy than can be found in those of any other manufacture.
BURTIS & GRAFF,
237 Water St., - - - - New York.

CAMPAIGN EQUIPMENTS.
N. EAMES & CO.,
46 West Broadway, New York City,
Manufacturers and Dealers in Banners, Caps, Capes, Torches, Shirts, Belts, Campaign Tenor Drums, Transparencies, Flags, Streamers, Bunting, Eames's "Official" Campaign Badge, Portraits of Candidates, in six oil colors (two by three feet) for Banners, Club Rooms, etc., Presidential Grand March Campaign Song Book, entirely new Campaign Songs, Fireworks, Colored Tableaux, Lights for Meeting nights, embracing more articles than all other dealers combined. Furnish latest patterns and designs at rates ten to fifty per cent. less than others in the business.

The **Eames's "Official" Campaign Badge,** adopted by the leading Clubs and political organizations in the Union—trade price, $12 per gross, net cash. Samples of each sent, postpaid, on receipt of 25 cents.

$12 net cash per gross.	$3.30 net cash per quarter gross.
$ 6.50 " " half gross.	Samples of each 25c., postpaid.

We offer greatly reduced rates on open-work Banners with candidates' Portraits in six oil colors. and have facilities for producing 100 Banners per day, at rates 25 per cent. less than other dealers. Send address on "postal" for mammoth Illustrated Sheet, containing *fac-simile* designs of our campaign goods in great variety, at reduced rates.

Clubs send address on "postal" and receive our Colored Circular. Special inducements offered Clubs or parties sending address on "postal" will receive our grand Supplement, issued September 1st and October 15th, containing over 100 designs of our goods. Do not delay, but send immediately.

N. EAMES & CO., 46 West Broadway, New York City.

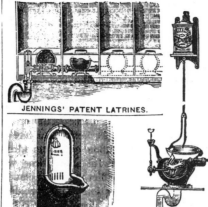
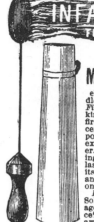

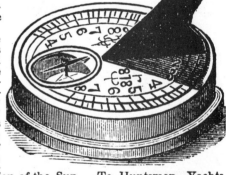

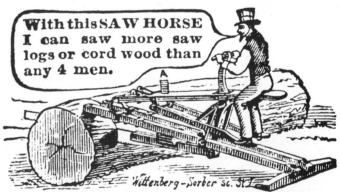

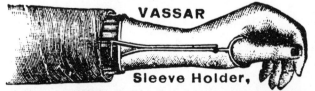

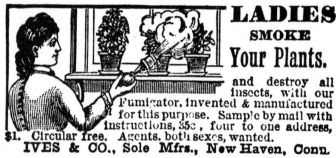
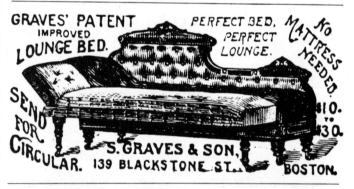

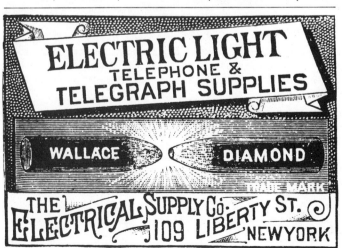

STEAM WASHER.

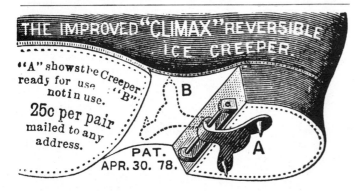

SPEAKING TELEPHONES.

THE AMERICAN BELL TELEPHONE COMPANY,

W. H. FORBES,	W. R. DRIVER,	THEO. N. VAIL,
President.	*Treasurer.*	*Gen. Manager.*

Alexander Graham Bell's patent of March 7, 1876, owned by this company, covers every form of apparatus, including Microphones or Carbon Telephones, in which the voice of the speaker causes electric undulations corresponding to the words spoken, and which articulations produce similar articulate sounds at the receiver. The Commissioner of Patents and the U. S. Circuit Court have decided this to be the true meaning of his claim; the validity of the patent has been sustained in the Circuit on final hearing in a contested case, and many injunctions and final decrees have been obtained on them.

This company also owns and controls all the other telephonic inventions of Bell, Edison, Berliner, Gray, Blake, Phelps, Watson, and others.

(Descriptive catalogues forwarded on application.)

Telephones for Private Line, Club, and Social systems can be procured directly or through the authorized agents of the company.

All telephones obtained except from this company, or its authorized licensees, are infringements, and the makers, sellers, and users will be proceeded against.

Information furnished upon application.

Address all communications to the

AMERICAN BELL TELEPHONE COMPANY,
95 Milk Street, Boston, Mass.

"THE BEST THING OF ALL FOR A CHRISTMAS BOX"

LUX-CO BOSTON

TELEPHONES SOLD.

Don't pay exorbitant rental fees to the Bell Telephone Monopoly to use their Telephones on lines less than two miles in length. A few months' rental buys a first-class Telephone that is no infringement, and works splendid on lines for private use on any kind of wire, and works good in stormy weather. It makes homes pleasant; annihilates time; prevents burglaries; saves many steps, and is just what every business man and farmer should have to connect stores, houses, depots, factories, colleges, etc., etc. The only practicable and reliable Telephone that is sold outright and warranted to work.

Chance for agents. No previous experience required. Circulars free. **WM. L. NORTON, Buffalo, N. Y.**

Automatic Transit Monthly ECLIPSE.

The figures in the Moon change 13 times. Size, 8 x 12 inches. 10,000 sold the first week. Agents Wanted. Sample postpaid for 17 cents. Seven for $1. **HIGH ART NOVELTY CO.,** St. Louis, Mo. Box 549.

AUTOMATIC
EYE-GLASS HOLDER

Winds up cord itself. "A" shows position of glasses reeled up. No breaking of glasses; very handy. Sold by Opticians. By mail. 25cts.

Ketcham & McDougall,
Manufacturers,
4 LIBERTY PLACE, N. Y.

THIS GREAT PREMIUM ABSOLUTELY FREE!
GOLD PLATED CASES

A STEM WINDER AND SETTER WITH GOLD PLATED CHAIN AND CHARM

THIS CUT IS EXACT SIZE AND PATTERN

CALLANDER, ENGRAVED, HUNTING CASES, PATENT AND ADJUSTMENT

Farm and Household, the well-known Literary and Farm Paper, now in its 5th year, has already over 100,000 subscribers, and is without question the most **popular farm and home paper** in the United States. It is elegantly printed and illustrated on fine paper, and its contributors are the ablest and best in each department that money can procure. It has been our custom each year to offer some great Premium, worth in itself many times more than the price of the paper, to secure new subscribers, knowing that if once subscribers they will never leave us, and **we propose to add 100,000 new subscribers during the next 6 months** if money and enterprise will accomplish it. This year we offer the premium illustrated above. It has beautiful Gold Plated Engraved Hunting Cases, is a stem-winder and stem-setter, with patent adjustment and stem-winding arrangement with Calendar, and tells the days of the month as well as the time of day. A gold plated Chain and Whistle Charm goes with each. It is entirely new, being patented Feb. 9, 1886, and will not be sold by watch dealers or jewelers. We own the patent exclusively and it can only be secured in connection with our paper. **HOW YOU CAN GET ONE FREE:** Send $1.00 in stamps, bill, money order or postal note for **one year's subscription to Farm and Household,** and we will send it in a nice Case with gold plated Chain and Whistle Charm **absolutely free and post-paid** as a premium. **THIS OFFER IS FOR NEW SUBSCRIBERS ONLY** and cannot be accepted by those already subscribers or any other member of their family. **WILL NOT BE SOLD SEPARATE.** As this Great Premium is intended solely to secure **new subscribers,** we will **not sell it at any price.** We give it away, and the only way you can secure it is to send $1.00 for one year's subscription to Farm and Household, when it will be sent you safely packed by return mail, Free and Post-paid as a premium. **References:** We have been so long before the public as enterprising contributors that we are well known to all newspaper publishers, and no doubt to most of their readers. Any Bank, Merchant, Publisher, or Express Agent in Connecticut can tell you of our absolute reliability. Address **PUBLISH'S FARM AND HOUSEHOLD, WALLINGFORD, CONN.**

THE FIRST
THE LARGEST   THE BEST

UNITED STATES MUTUAL ACCIDENT ASSOCIATION

NEW FEATURES:

$10,000 Death by Accident.
$10,000 Loss Hands or Feet.
$10,000   "   Hand and Foot.
$5,000   "   Hand or Foot.
$5,000   "   Both Eyes.
$1,300   "   One Eye.
$2,500 Permanent Total Disability.
$50 a Week Temporary Total   "

These amounts of Indemnity are provided by the Policies of the UNITED STATES MUTUAL ACCIDENT ASSOCIATION, 320 and 322 Broadway, N. Y., at a cost to members in the preferred occupations of about $26 a year, which may be made in one payment or in installments.

One-half or one-quarter of above insurance at proportionate rates. Membership Fee, $5 for each $5,000 Policy.

CHAS. B. PEET, Prest.
JAS. R. PITCHER,
Sec. & Gen. M'g'r.

This cut represents laying over rough boards our

RUBBER ROOFING.

Costs only $3.25 per square, 10 x 10 feet, and will last a lifetime on steep or flat roofs.
Send *at once* for Book Circular. References and samples free, if you *mention* this paper.

INDIANA PAINT AND ROOFING CO., 143 DUANE STREET, N.Y.

$5. COUNTY RIGHTS. $5.

The Eastlake Clothes Stick. Bauder's Pat., March, 1879. Saves both time and labor, while the operator receives no scalds. Novel in construction, perfect in operation. Sells everywhere. Price 25 cts. Costs about 2 cts.—profits, 1,200 per cent. County rights—outside of Ohio—for sale (good for 16 years). Price only FIVE Dollars, including sample, prepaid. Refer to our P. M. and County Commissioners. Address
BAUDER & CO., Birmingham, Erie Co., Ohio.

EVERY FAMILY
Should have our new
PATENT EXTENSION
Duplex Lamp
with the
Evening Umbrella,
FOR LIGHTING
Libraries and Pianos.
The only perfect light for this purpose.
Send for Circular.
Mention Companion.

R. HOLLINGS & CO., Manufacturers & Importers,
547 Washington Street, BOSTON, MASS.

HYPNOTISM

The Wonder Of the Age.

Now is the time to take up Hypnotism. Do you know what marvelous strides it has lately made? Are you aware that it now stands as a vigorous and harmonious science—that the world's greatest scholars are keenly watching its developments—that it is proving itself the "right bower" of education and justice, of medicine and reform—and that hypnotists, in fine, seem personally to hold a leadership among their fellow mortals and the keys to riches, health and happiness? All this has been the progress of a very few years, and to those who desire a money-making and honorable profession the whole subject is one of most intense interest. Time was when this mysterious science held timid souls aloof. As things are now going it will soon be a positive danger *not* to know Hypnotism, and how to use its powers. The case is admirably stated in a FREE BOOK just published by the renowned Prof. L. A. Harraden. This book is called a "Key to the Mysteries of Hypnotism." It is the clearest, most complete and graphic review of the subject ever written. It explains the mysteries of Hypnotism from A to Z. It tells you just what Hypnotism is and what it will accomplish. It tells you how you may sway the minds of others, perform astounding feats, and produce amusement by the hour. The Professor is a thorough expert as well as a famous teacher, and he knows how to impart his facts in a clear and pleasing manner. What he doesn't know about Hypnotism you may be sure is not worth knowing. The mechanical features of the book are worthy of its precious contents. The Professor has spared no expense on it, for he wishes those who get a copy to treasure it and to read it. Besides being elegantly printed, it is adorned on every page with choice illustrations relating to the text. These cost considerable money, and some are surprised that the Professor gives away his book without charging one cent. It is free, nevertheless, to all who drop him a line by letter or postal. He is determined that the masses shall have a chance to learn Hypnotism, and to know how it heals the sick, cures vicious habits, wins influence, position, love, friendship. wealth and happiness. Write for a copy of this FREE BOOK, and read it at once. You will never get such a chance in your life again. Address.

Prof. L. A. HARRADEN. Dept. 18, Jackson, Michigan.

Air-Tight Rubber Tip
PEARL MUCILAGE.

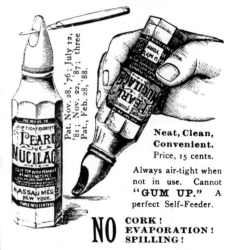

Pat. Nov. 28, '76; July 12, '81; Nov. 22, '87; three Pat, Feb. 28, '88.

Neat, Clean, Convenient.
Price, 15 cents.

Always air-tight when not in use. Cannot "GUM UP." A perfect Self-Feeder.

NO CORK! EVAPORATION! SPILLING!

Sample by mail on receipt of **20 CENTS.** For sale by stationers.

THE NASSAU MFG. CO., 140 Nassau St., New York.

The Best Mucilage in the Best Bottle.

THE PANSY SEWING MACHINE, $3.50.

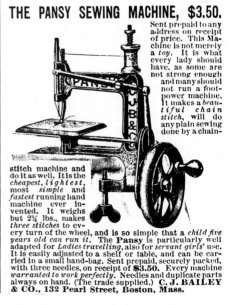

Sent prepaid to any address on receipt of price. This Machine is not merely a *toy*. It is what every lady should have, as some are not strong enough and many should not run a foot-power machine. It makes a *beautiful chain stitch*, will do any plain sewing done by a chain-stitch machine and do it as well. It is the *cheapest, lightest,* most *simple* and *fastest* running hand machine ever invented. It weighs but 2¼ lbs., makes *three stitches* to every turn of the wheel, and is so simple that a *child five years old can run it.* The Pansy is particularly well adapted for *Ladies travelling,* also for *servant girls'* use. It is easily adjusted to a shelf or table, and can be carried in a small hand-bag. Sent prepaid, securely packed, with three needles, on receipt of **$3.50.** Every machine *warranted to work perfectly.* Needles and duplicate parts always on hand. (The trade supplied.) C. J. BAILEY & CO., 132 Pearl Street, Boston, Mass.

A SENSIBLE DOCTOR.

"What! worn out with your housekeeping? You do not need me, then; you need rest!"
(After which wise remark he continued his discourse as follows:)
"Do not deceive yourself by thinking that everything in the house can be done better by yourself than your good servant. In many cases she might, indeed, not equal your efficiency; but if you are always careful to provide her with Sapolio, she cannot fail to keep everything about your house as clean and bright as it is possible to make it." (And then he laughed heartily:) "Ha! ha! I might as well add that Sapolio only costs a few cents per cake, and my visits come somewhat higher."

1885–1890/95

Necessity is the mother of invention. With the growing use of polished brass, nickel and steel articles in domestic interiors came the discovery of Stilboma, to make and keep them bright. Stilboma is a chemically prepared chamois, which polishes or burnishes metal surfaces. It is neat, clean and durable—and never scratches.

A large sample of Stilboma will be sent to anyone who will mention where this advertisement was seen and enclose six cents in stamps to THE CHANDLER & RUDD CO., Cleveland, Ohio

Rogers, Peet & Co., of New York City, invite requests for a leaflet "Bathing without Fear," descriptive of a unique bathing suit and life-preserver combined ; for men, women and children.

ARCHER'S BARBER CHAIR No. 13.

Gynecological, Dentist and Barber Chairs. Piano and Store Stools. Six (6) new Styles of Barber Chairs out May 1st. Send for catalogue. ARCHER MFG. CO., Rochester, N.Y., U.S.A.

The Johnny Green Bank.

Given for one new name, and 10 cts. additional.

This is a great attraction to the young people ; beside, it will encourage them to save their pennies. Deposit a penny in the Bank, and the fun begins.

A boy rings the bell, while he is supposed to ask for the naughty boy who so cruelly deposited the cat in the well.

Little Johnny Green, flourishing his hat and sitting on the fence, is, no doubt, the guilty party.

Jack Stout then actually extracts poor pussy from the well—brave boy. The clockwork moves the figures in a very life-like manner.

Given for one new name, and 10 cts. additional. Price, $1. Postage and packing, 20 cts., when sent as a premium or purchased.

Copyrighted 1890 *by Lum Smith's Agents' Herald, Phila., Pa.*

SPECIAL BILL POSTERS WANTED

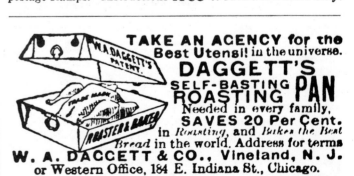

A Special Messenger leaves the Phila. P.O. every 15 minutes with ALL of LUM SMITH'S Mail in a *locked* pouch. Distance to Smith's Office, two blocks.

Advertisers, Patentees, Manufacturers, etc., are continually requesting us to supply the addresses of reliable circular distributers, bill posters, etc. Brunn's success is marvelous, and will open up in 200,000 HERALDS next month, to be mailed to business firms, a new, profitable and permanent business to one man, woman or youth in every town in the U. S. and Canada. "The early bird catches the worm." We want a few such "ads." as Brunn's to start with in next month's MAMMOTH editions of the AGENTS' HERALD.

Brunn paid $2.40 to insert 4 lines, June '90 He began during summer. That ad. paid then; *is paying now.* He has been kept constantly busy, employs three men to assist him, clearing *on their labor* from $10 to $15 a day distributing circulars at $1 per 1000 for many firms who saw his ad. in the HERALD. It costs every firm at least $10 in postage alone to mail 1000 circulars. **You** advertise to **hand them** out for $1 per 1000. A saving to each firm who employs you of $9 per 1000. **Parents** make your boys a present. Start them in this growing business. Begin this neat business before some one in your county gets the start of you. "Come in on the ground floor." 4 lines as below (Brunn's) in 200,000 HERALDS costs $2.40 ; 3 lines as below (Foster's) $1.80 ; 2 lines as below (Best's) $1.20 ; cash or postage stamps. Instructions **free** to such advertisers only.

TAKE AN AGENCY for the Best Utensil in the universe. DAGGETT'S SELF-BASTING ROASTING PAN Needed in every family. SAVES 20 Per Cent. in *Roasting*, and *Bakes the Best Bread* in the world. Address for terms W. A. DAGGETT & CO., Vineland, N. J. or Western Office, 184 E. Indiana St., Chicago.

THE VICTOR TYPE-WRITER

EXCELS IN SPEED, IN QUALITY OF WORK, IN DURABILITY.

A Perfect Machine.   Very Simple.   Easy to Learn.

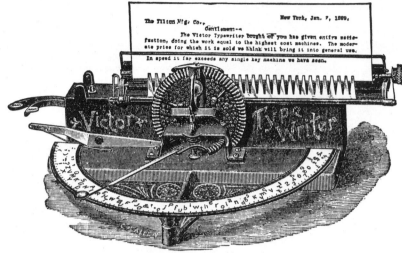

PRICE, $15.00.

The **VICTOR** is now being rapidly introduced throughout the United States, and we offer liberal inducements and exclusive territory to Agents wishing to sell the best Single-Keyed Type-writer made.

WRITE FOR PARTICULARS.

GEORGE D. JOHNSON, GENERAL AGENT FOR NEW ENGLAND.
7 MILK STREET, BOSTON, MASS

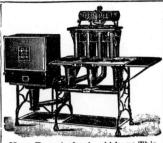
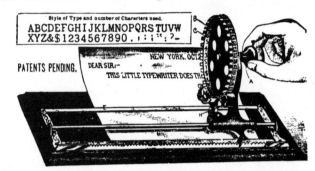

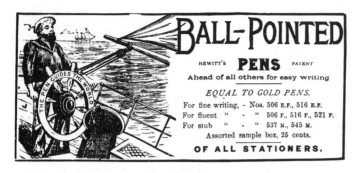

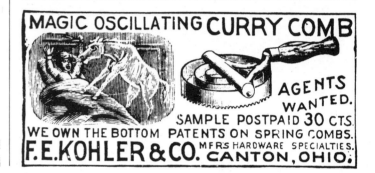

The TYPEWRITER.

Dollar $1

This Typewriter has an automatic feed and a self-inking type wheel, uses copying ink, will accommodate the largest sized letter paper, and possesses many of the features of a higher cost machine. It will write a neat letter, with considerable speed and for addressing envelopes, is especially useful. It is a great educator for the young, teaching spelling, composition and punctuation, besides being very amusing and fascinating. 48 page Catalogue FREE or sent with the Typewriter by express for $1.00; by mail 15c. extra. Size, 3x4x9 inch. SATISFACTION GUARANTEED. Agts. wanted. **ROBT. H. INGERSOLL & BRO. 65 CORTLANDT ST. N. Y. CITY.**

New method of making Ice Cream
SHEPARD'S "LIGHTNING" FREEZER
WHEEL DASHER.　　　　CEDAR TUB.
Freezes much the quickest and easiest, also makes most Ice Cream.
SHEPARD HARDWARE Co.
BUFFALO, N.Y.
Shepard's "Lighting" Freezer Receipt Book Mailed Free.

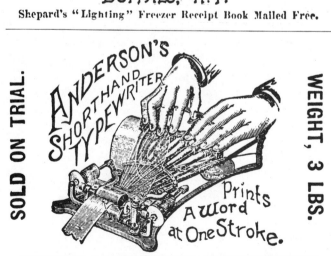

SOLD ON TRIAL.

ANDERSON'S SHORTHAND TYPEWRITER

Prints A Word at One Stroke.

WEIGHT, 3 LBS.

REQUIRES NO KNOWLEDGE OF STENOGRAPHY.

Six weeks' practice assures a speed of **100 words a minute** Now used for all kinds of short-hand work. If not sold by your local business college, send for circular and keep up with the times. **Price, complete, $30.**
R. RUSH & BRO.,
245 Broadway, New York City.

AUSABLE

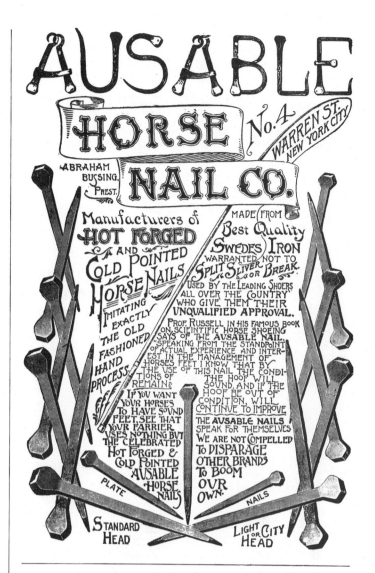

HORSE No. 4
WARREN ST. NEW YORK CITY

ABRAHAM BUSSING, PREST.

NAIL CO.

Manufacturers of **HOT FORGED** AND **COLD POINTED HORSE NAILS** IMITATING EXACTLY THE OLD FASHIONED HAND PROCESS.

MADE FROM Best Quality SWEDES IRON WARRANTED NOT TO SPLIT SLIVER OR BREAK.

USED BY THE LEADING SHOERS ALL OVER THE COUNTRY WHO GIVE THEM THEIR UNQUALIFIED APPROVAL.

PROF. RUSSELL IN HIS FAMOUS BOOK ON SCIENTIFIC HORSE SHOEING SAYS OF THE AUSABLE NAIL. "SPEAKING FROM THE STANDPOINT OF ACTUAL EXPERIENCE AND INTEREST IN THE MANAGEMENT OF HORSES FEET I KNOW THAT BY THE USE OF THIS NAIL THE CONDITIONS OF THE HOOF WILL REMAIN. SOUND AND IF THE HOOF BE OUT OF CONDITION, WILL CONTINUE TO IMPROVE

IF YOU WANT YOUR HORSES TO HAVE SOUND FEET, SEE THAT YOUR FARRIER USES NOTHING BUT THE CELEBRATED HOT FORGED & COLD POINTED AUSABLE HORSE NAILS.

THE AUSABLE NAILS SPEAK FOR THEMSELVES WE ARE NOT COMPELLED TO DISPARAGE OTHER BRANDS TO BOOM OUR OWN.

PLATE　　NAILS

STANDARD HEAD　　LIGHT OR CITY HEAD

THE NEW MODEL "HALL."

A Perfect Typewriter. Best Manifolder. Terms to Agents liberal. Portable, Inexpensive. Writes all languages. *Read Mr. Howells' opinion:*
"I wish to express my very great satisfaction with the Hall Typewriter. Impressions and alignment are both more perfect than any other typewriter that I know, and it is simply a pleasure to use it. It is delightfully simple and manageable." (Signed) W. D. HOWELLS.
Send for Catalogue and Specimens of Work.
Address N. TYPEWRITER CO., 8 Temple Pl., Boston.

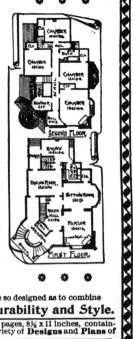

FISKE'S AMATEUR'S BOOT AND SHOE REPAIRING JACK

will repair any shoe from a child's size 10 to a man's 11. Boys, repair your own shoes at home, also your father's, mother's, sisters', brothers' and cousins' and aunts' (if they will pay for it). Any boy from 12 to 15 years old can do it with our Jack and outfit; price, $8.25, which consists of one Repairing Jack, $2.50; one doz. pairs white oak Half Soles, $1.75; one doz. pairs Heel Lifts, 60c.; one pat. Peg Awl Haft, 10c.; half doz. Peg Awls, 5c.; three sewing Awls and Handles, 15c.; one Ball Thread, 10c.; one Box Ink Powder, 10c.; three qts. Pegs, 15c.; one ℔. wire Clinch Nails, 15c.; one ℔. Heel Nails, 5c.; one ℔. steel Nails, 10c.; one pair Pinchers, 50c.; one Hammer, 25c.; one Shoe Knife, 20c.; one Emery Knife Sharpener, 25c.; one Burnisher, 35c.; fifty pairs Star Plates, 50c.; half doz. Shoe-makers' Needles, 5c.; one Stick Heel Ball, 10c.; one Bottle Leather Cement, 10c.; one Bottle Rubber Cement, 15c.; one Rasp and Wax, 40c. These Half Soles and Heels are all cut out with dies, ready to put on, and are of the best white oak leather, all sizes. The stock included in the outfit will make from $12.00 to $15.00 worth of work, and you have the Jack and Tools left for more work. Price, $8.25. Will send this entire outfit by Express, C. O. D., subject to your approval, or by Freight, upon receipt of the price, $8.25. Full instructions go with every outfit. We also manufacture Fiske's Oil and Rubber Patent Leather Polish. A sample bottle goes with every outfit. Price, $1.25 per doz. The outfit weighs 50 lbs. If you order by Express, C. O. D., send $2.00 on account. We pay charges on money returned. The tools and Stock in this outfit are of the finest quality and the same as we sell our regular trade. Correspondence solicited.

J. D. FISKE & CO.,
Wholesale Dealers in Leather and Findings,
278 Asylum St.,   Hartford, Conn.

PRESS THE BUTTON, IT LIGHTS!

Half a million in daily use. The only practical self-lighting pocket device; a bright light from a minute to an hour at any instant. Invaluable to the smoker and sportsman. It fits your vest pocket in size and price. Expressed, prepaid, complete with accessories, to any address in the U. S. or Canada, on receipt of $1. Write for circular of Magic Novelties to MAGIC INTRODUCTION COMPANY, 227 Broadway, New York. Agents Wanted.

THE HUMAN HAND as seen through the **WONDER-TUBE** X-Ray effects shown **without Electricity or Crookes Tube.** Rainbow colors at night. No mirrors used. Price of Tube, 10 cts. by mail. Wonder-Tube Co., 925 F St., Washington, D.C.

Portable X Ray Apparatus

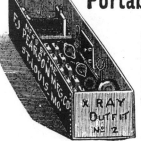

Our No. 2 Outfit for Physicians, Professors, Photographers, and Students. Complete in handsome case, including coil, condenser, 2 sets tubes, battery, etc. Price, $15, net, delivered in U. S. Guaranteed highest class apparatus.
F. J. PEARSON MFG. CO.
Main & Locust Sts.,
St. Louis, Mo.

FASTER THAN SHORTHAND!

Anderson's Shorthand Typewriter *prints a word at one stroke!* Price, $25. It is a perfect substitute for stenography, and has already taken its place in many of the largest establishments in the country. You can learn at home without a teacher; no knowledge of shorthand necessary. Begin practice NOW and you will be ready for WORK next month. S. G. K. Anderson, 50 Chestnut St., Newark, N. J. New York Office, 291 Broadway.

No. 37
Spencerian
Vertical Steel Pens.

Spencerian Steel Pens

Long experience, together with the utmost care in their manufacture, have secured absolute uniformity of quality, which entitles them to their standing amongst expert penmen, correspondents and accountants as The Best.

Six Sample Vertical Pens sent on receipt of four cents in postage-stamps. Ask for No. 37.

SPENCERIAN PEN CO.,
450 Broome St., New York, N. Y.

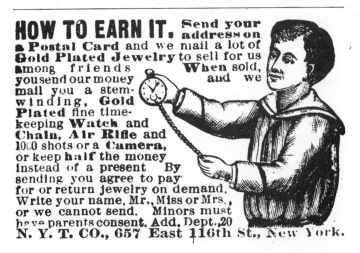

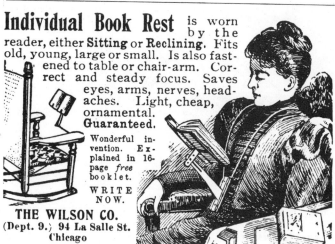

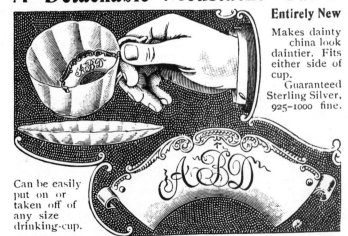

HYPNOTISM
DOES IT PAY? FREE!

That is the chief question for the practical reader. Everybody admits that it is an interesting and wonderful science. It is the only science existing that penetrates to the hidden and inscrutable recesses of thought. Its grasp is on the **MIND** as that of the physical sciences is on **MATTER.** It deals with the unseen, the intangible, the mysterious. But, you ask, does it pay to learn it? Does it pay to know it? Does it pay to acquire its methods and practice it as an art or calling? I at once answer you, yes, emphatically, YES. Just apply to it the same tests that you would to any other business, craft or calling. Why do you study any of them? Is it not to earn a living, to provide for your family, to secure an independence, to obtain friends, distinction and happiness for yourself and your loved ones? It certainly is; these are the objects in life that men strive and toil for, and I tell you that Hypnotism offers a surer and speedier way to obtain them than any other means open to the rising generation. This is true, and I will give you the best proof of it. I will give you for the asking a copy of **MY FREE BOOK,** which is entitled, a "Key to the Mysteries of Hypnotism," but is likewise a triumphant answer to the question, "Does it pay?" This is a book of elegant appearance, richly illustrated on every page, and is certainly the nicest book ever given away free in the interests of science. It cost me much time, labor and money, but it will cost you nothing whatever but the trouble of writing for it, even on a postal card, if need be. As the title implies, my book tells you all about Hypnotism, its history, development, methods, phenomena and uses, but flashing out of every line you will also learn the secret of how it pays. In the first place, it is easy and quick to learn, easier than any other study which forms the basis of a livilihood or profession. Anybody who can merely read can master it quickly, and then will never forget it. Surely that is a paying feature to the youth starting out in life, to the bread-winner who desires a change for the better, or anybody needing an honorable and lucrative profession. Compare it, if you like, with the years spent in college to learn law or medicine, or the years of apprenticeship to a trade or business. But Hypnotism also PAYS PROMPTLY in this one grand feature, it gives you control of other minds and direction of their wills. You may not at once see what that amounts to. Send for and read my book, FREE, and you will find that this mental dominion is a passport to social favor, to public reputation, to advancement in position, and to the highest success in business. Control of other minds is not only thus a fortune-winner, but my book will show you how it works to banish pain, to cure every known disease or bad habit, to correct either moral or intellectual frailty, to win ardent love and devoted friendship, to benefit, to bless and to entertain all around you, not only for instant gain, but for a continuance of health, prosperity and happiness. Now, if I prove all this, won't you admit that IT PAYS? Well, my book proves it. It costs you nothing to get it. It is a master-key to all the treasure vaults of life. Write for it this very hour, and learn the knowledge that all this world's a-seeking. IT IS FREE. Address, **Prof. L. A. HARRADEN, Jackson. Michigan.**

BEAUTY

THE EMPRESS BELT.

FOR LADIES AND CHILDREN.

From HARPER'S BAZAAR: "*A Metallic Belt, called the Empress, finished in jet, silvered, gilt and plaid patterns, and worn with slides to match, is convenient and pretty with morning wrappers. It is also useful as a foundation for Silk Belts.*" Samples sent by mail, post-paid, on receipt of $1. Be particular to give size of waist.

Address   EMPRESS METALLIC BELT CO.
153 CHAMBERS STREET, NEW YORK.

ANTI-FAT

The GREAT REMEDY for
CORPULENCE.

ALLAN'S ANTI-FAT

Is purely vegetable and perfectly harmless. It acts upon the food in the stomach, preventing its being converted into fat. Taken in accordance with directions, **it will reduce a fat person from two to five pounds per week.**

"Corpulence is not only a disease itself, but the harbinger of others." So wrote Hippocrates two thousand years ago, and what was true then is none the less so to-day.

Sold by druggists, or sent, by express, upon receipt of $1.50. Quarter-dozen $4.00. Address,

BOTANIC MEDICINE CO.,
Proprietors, Buffalo, N. Y.

Fashions for 1867.
J. W. BRADLEY'S
DUPLEX ELLIPTIC
(OR DOUBLE)
SPRING SKIRTS.

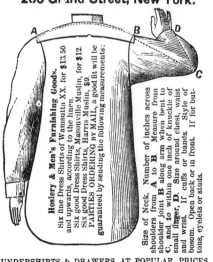

They will not BEND or BREAK like the SINGLE SPRINGS, but will PRESERVE their PERFECT and GRACEFUL SHAPE, in all CROWDED Assemblages, CHURCHES, THEATRES, RAILROAD CARS, and for Promenade or House Dress, where three or four ordinary skirts are THROWN ASIDE as USELESS!

EACH HOOP is composed of TWO FINELY-TEMPERED Steel Springs, BRAIDED TIGHTLY and FIRMLY together, EDGE to EDGE, forming one Hoop, thus making the STRONGEST and MOST FLEXIBLE, as well as the MOST DURABLE and STYLISH SKIRT EVER MADE. In fact, they are superior to all others COMBINING COMFORT, ECONOMY, LIGHTNESS, ELEGANCE and DURABILITY. THIS POPULAR SKIRT is UNIVERSALLY RECOMMENDED by the FASHION MAGAZINES and OPINIONS of the PRESS generally. At WHOLESALE by the exclusive Manufacturers and Sole Owners of the Patent,

WESTS, BRADLEY & CARY,
Warerooms and Office, Nos. 97 Chambers Street, and 79 & 81 Reade St., New York. Also at Wholesale by the Leading Jobbers.   tf-o

---

J. W. JOHNSTON,
260 Grand Street, New York.

Hosiery & Men's Furnishing Goods.
Six fine Dress Shirts of Wamsutta XX. for $13.50 and upwards, according to the linen.
Six good Dress Shirts, Masonville Muslin, for $12.
Six good Dress Shirts, Harris Muslin, $9.
PARTIES ORDERING BY MAIL, a good fit will be guaranteed by sending the following measurements:

Size of Neck. Number of inches across shoulders from **A** to **B**. Measure from **A** to **B** along arm when bent to **C**, and to within one inch of knuckle of small finger, **D**. Size around chest, waist and wrist. If cuffs or bands. Style of bosom. Open back or in front. If for buttons, eyelets or studs.

UNDERSHIRTS & DRAWERS AT POPULAR PRICES.

ASCOUGH'S PAREPA HOOD.

For elegance of design, perfect finish, and fineness of material, this fashionable Hood is unrivaled. It is ornamented with crystals which produce a very novel and beautiful effect. It is suitable to all ages, and is adjustable at pleasure. It gives beauty to youth, and comeliness to middle age. It is also adapted to all seasons, and fit for Sleighing, Skating, Traveling, the Opera or the Promenade. Manufactured only by WILLIAM ASCOUGH, Buffalo. For sale wholesale and retail by

A. T. STEWART & CO., New York.,
AND BY ALL FIRST HOUSES THROUGHOUT THE COUNTRY.

HARRIS' (PATENT) PREVOST
SIDE CUT
KID GLOVES.

Entirely New and Elegant!

This cut of Glove is entirely new and different from all others, the buttons being scarcely perceptible when the arm is raised, while the peculiar and perfect fit adds to the natural beauty and symmetry of the arm. It renders the Glove easier to put on, and is more agreeable to the hand and arm.

These Gloves come in 4, 6, 8, and 10 buttons, in White and in all the delicate light shades for Parties, Balls, Opera, and Receptions. To be obtained only of

HARRIS BROTHERS,
877 BROADWAY,

Between 18th & 19th Sts.,   New York.
Write for Sample Color Card, which will be promptly forwarded free of charge.

FOR
MOTH PATCHES,
FRECKLES and TAN,
USE
PERRY'S
MOTH & FRECKLE
LOTION.

It is reliable and harmless.

Depot, 49 Bond Street,
NEW YORK.

Sold by Druggists everywhere.

 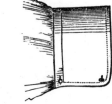

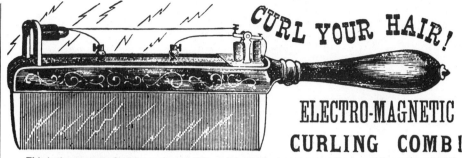
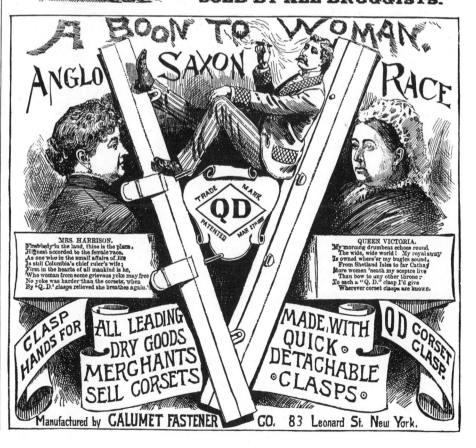

The "Seamless" Parasol.
SEASON 1884.

The "Seamless" Parasol is characterized by a square centre, made of one piece, and not cut into breadths as is usual in umbrellas and parasols. The style has not merely novelty to recommend it, but it is especially adapted to figured fabrics which can be displayed without the distortion incident to cutting into eight, ten, or more breadths, according to the number of ribs. The parasol is finished by a flounce, which may be of the same or different material, and the junction between this flounce and the square centre is concealed by a simple ruching. Lace or fringe can both be used for trimming. The possible variations in this "Seamless" style are very great, and an opportunity is given to use fabrics not ordinarily adapted for parasols. With crape for the centre it makes a mourning parasol of great elegance, and it is equally well adapted for a bridal parasol of pure white silk or satin, with a centre covering of lace.

WM. A. DROWN & CO., Manufacturers,
Frankford, Philadelphia, Pa.

I ALWAYS KNOW A GENTLEMAN. HE GETS HIS BOOTS BLACKED AND WEARS CLOTHING FROM ROGERS PEET & CO. 487 BROADWAY NEW YORK.

Persons at a distance should write for Samples and Directions for ordering

MEN'S AND BOYS' CLOTHING.

"OUR PERFECT."

Perfect

TO KNOW
how to clothe the
CHILDREN
BOYS,
GIRLS,
BABIES

In the latest styles and best manner at the least trouble and expense, send for the

Liliputian Bazaar
CATALOGUE
Which we mail free.

Our **"Perfect"** waists are incomparably the best in the world. They support the clothing directly from the shoulder, and will be found indispensable for their comfort and hygienic value to a growing child. We send them for trial subject to return for refund of money if not satisfactory.

Everything for Children's wear from Hats to Shoes.

BEST & CO. 60 W. 23d Street, Bet. 5th & 6th Aves. N.Y.

There, Nellie, what did I tell you, you have just ruined that new dress under the arms because you did not have a Canfield Dress Shield.

THE CANFIELD
Patent, "Elastic Seamless"
DRESS SHIELDS

are waterproof, absorbent, odorless, strong, yet soft as kid, do not wrinkle, chafe or rip, are easily shaped to the garment and only *seamless* shield made. This is a recent American invention and the sales are already double that of any other Dress Protector made in Europe or United States. These goods are protected by patents and trade marks all over the world.

Beware of imitations. All genuine goods bear the trade mark shown above.

The Canfield Rubber Co., Middletown, Conn.

THERE CHARLIE, DON'T CRY, BUT GIVE THIS CARD TO YOUR FATHER AND HE CAN SEND TO ROGERS PEET & CO'S CLOTHING STORE, AT 487 BROADWAY NEW YORK AND GET YOU A NICE SUIT OF CLOTHES.

We dress Our Daughters in "Nonpareil" Velveteen. John Mrs. Bull

NONPAREIL

WHOLESALE AGENTS SHAEN & FITHIAN. NEW YORK

Take no Substitute for the GENUINE
H. T. MARSHALL'S
Patent Adjustable
Lace Congress
IN HIGH OR LOW CUT.

A Congress that will not draw the foot. A Lace Boot that requires no lacing in putting on or off. It has all the merits of both, and is an improvement on either Shoe.

PRICE,
$3.50 to $7.

WARRANTED IF BOTTOM IS STAMPED MAY 13. 1884. H. T. MARSHALL. PAT'D. PAT. STAMP WOVEN IN STRAP OF EACH SHOE.

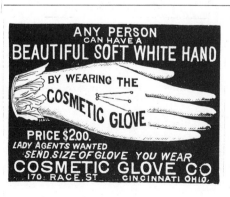

PEARS' SOAP

·a·Specialty·for·Children·

The Double Ve Waist

PAT. NOV. 10TH 1885.

FOR **BOYS** AND **GIRLS** ages 3 to 12 yrs.
SUPPORTS stockings and underclothes from
the **SHOULDERS. No stiff cords.** *No useless*
harness to bother. Fits beautifully and with perfect
ease and freedom. Will **WASH.** Wears splen-
didly. **Best and Cheapest.** Try one. For sale
everywhere. Sample by mail, **75 cents. FOY,**
HARMON & CHADWICK, New Haven, Conn.

FARGO'S "BOX TIP"

School Shoes for Boys and Girls

PRICES:

Sizes—8 to 10½	$1.25
" 11 to 13½	1.50
" 1 to 2	1.75

AND

$2.50 CALF.

TRADE MARK.

FARGO'S $2.50 SHOE

Congress, Button and Lace,
FOR MEN AND BOYS.

Our name is on the bottom of every shoe.
☞ Ask your Dealer for Fargo's "Box Tip"
and $2.50 Shoes. If he does not keep them,
send to us and we will send you a pair by
return mail, prepaid, on receipt of price.
If you try one pair of our shoes, and for any reason
they are not satisfactory, we will allow you to
return them and we will refund your money.
If you do not know what size to order, send to us for
directions for measuring. A Handsome Calendar
for 1889 sent with each order.
C. H. FARGO & CO., Chicago, Ill.
Name THE YOUTH'S COMPANION every time you write.

BEFORE AFTER BEFORE AFTER

DYKE'S BEARD ELIXIR
Forces Heavy Moustache, Massive Whis-
kers, and Hair on Bald Heads in 20 to 30
days. The only remedy. Extra strong. 2 or
3 pkgs. do it. We prove this or pay $100.00.
Just think, we send $1 size Pkgs. for 25c.
or 4 pkgs. each $1 size, mailed for 48c. in stamps.
Smith Mfg. Co. Palatine, Ills.

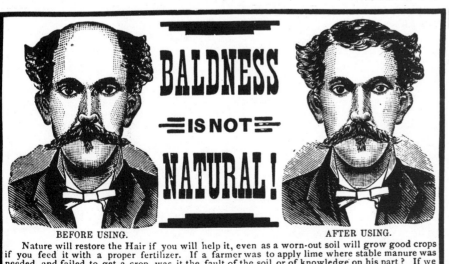

MADAME DEAN'S SPINAL SUPPORTING CORSETS.

They support the Spine, relieve the muscles of the back, brace the shoulders in a natural and easy manner, imparting graceful carriage to the wearer without discomfort, expanding the chest, thereby giving full action to the lungs, and health and comfort to the body. Take the place of the ORDINARY CORSET in every respect, and are made of fine Coutil, in the best manner, in various styles and sold by agents everywhere at popular prices. Mrs. Wm. Papes, Keota, Iowa, says:—I have been an invalid for six years, have travelled extensively for health, yet never received as much benefit as I have in a few weeks wear, of your MADAME DEAN'S CORSET. I am gaining strength all the time, and could not do without it. It has proven to me a *godsend.*

FREE Our new book entitled: "Dress Reform for Ladies" with elegant wood engraving and Biography of **Worth**, the King of Fashion, Paris; also our **New Illustrated Catalogue** sent **free** to any address on receipt of two 2-cent stamps to pay postage and packing.

AGENTS WANTED for these **celebrated Corsets.** No experience required. Four orders per day give the agent **$150 monthly.** Our agents report from four to twenty sales daily. **$3.00** outfit. Send at once for terms and full particulars. ⟨ **SCHIELE & CO.,** 390 Broadway, New York.

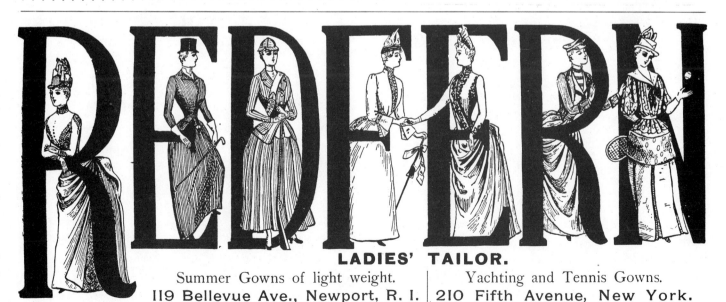

FOR CORRECT STYLES IN
Trimmed Millinery, Suits, Wraps, Etc.,
See the Spring and Summer

Great Double Number
RIDLEYS'
Fashion Magazine.

Over 2,000 Illustrations of everything necessary
for personal wear or adornment.

**Contains lowest New York prices
for each article and instruction
how to shop in New York.**

Sample Copies only 15 cents.

EDW. RIDLEY & SONS,

Grand, Orchard and Allen Sts., N. Y.

REDFERN,

By Appointment — To Her Majesty the Queen

Costumes Designed By Redfern for the Coming Season.

SPRING 1889.

MESSRS. JOHN REDFERN & SONS have the honor of
announcing to their lady-patrons that their arrangements for the ensuing season are now complete.

The ORIGINAL Models of Gowns, Coats and Hats,

designed and produced by them at their branches in NEW YORK, LONDON, COWES and PARIS

can be seen IN THEIR ENTIRETY, together with the largest stock of IMPORTED and

EXCLUSIVE CLOTHS in the United States, at their Showrooms,

210 Fifth Avenue, Through to 1132 Broadway, N. Y.

THE
COMING WOMAN
MUST BE
BEAUTIFUL.

The fashionable "fad" is Physical Culture for Women. If you can't belong to a gymnasium, have one at home. Special work for ladies and invalids designed by a well-known physician. You *can lift a ton a minute* without fatigue, and become graceful and handsome. Send stamp for illustrated pamphlets, "How we Trained Our Children," "How to Cure Disease by Exercise," "How to Get Strong."

STAR EXERCISER CO.

710 Broadway, N. Y.

The Shawknit Stockings,

Containing no bunches and no perceptible seams, constructed with reference to the shape of the human foot, and knitted from the best of yarns, are the nicest-fitting, longest-wearing, and most comfortable stockings ever put on the market. Coarse, Fine & Extra-fine (half-hose) in solid colors and mixtures, for men and youths; Super-stout (hose) in black for boys and girls.

None genuine unless stamped

This is the Heel — The Shawknit

on the toe. For sale by the trade generally.

☞ *Send for Descriptive Post-Paid Parcel Price-List to*
SHAW STOCKING CO., Lowell, Mass.

126/1885–1890

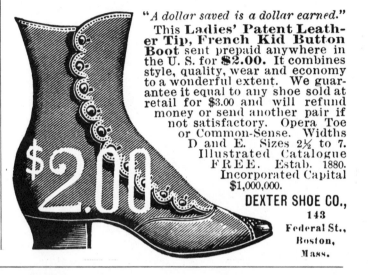

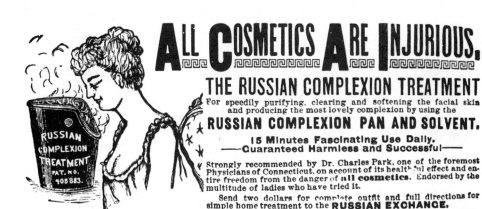

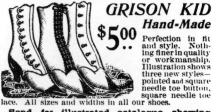

He (economical husband): SEE HERE, SIR! MY WIFE BOUGHT THESE GLOVES YESTERDAY AND THE FINGER ENDS ARE THROUGH ALREADY!

Practical Storekeeper: SHE DID NOT BUY THE RIGHT KIND! WE SELL THE "KAYSER PATENT FINGER TIPPED SILK GLOVES," AND WITH EVERY PAIR GIVE A "GUARANTEE TICKET" ENTITLING HER TO ANOTHER PAIR, *free of charge,* WHENEVER THE "TIPS" *fail to outwear the gloves.*

These Three Special Ladies' Cloaks
$6.00, $7.50 and $10.00

Cannot be duplicated anywhere under $10, $15, and $20. Send for one, also our

Handsome Cloak and Fur Catalogue
showing a hundred other styles.

No. 12, $7.50	No. 13, $10.00	No. 14, $6.00
Ladies' Jacket, sizes 32 to 44, made of very fine Black Bouclé, latest style fancy tucked sleeves trimmed with Round Crochet buttons, cloth facing, silk stitching; 27 inches long; would be cheap at $15. Same in Navy Blue, . . . $7.50 Same in Fine Navy Blue Beav'r 7.50 Same in Fine Black Beaver, 7.50	Ladies' Double Plush Cape, sizes 32 to 44, of Very High Grade Silk Seal Plush; Collar and Top Cape edged with Genuine Black Thibet Fur; both Capes lined with excellent Black Serge Silk; 28 inches long; others would ask $20.	Ladies' Double Cape, sizes 32 to 44 of very good quality black wool Beaver Cloth—upper cape trimmed with straps of same cloth—cloth straps edged with flat silk braid and set off, with Black Satin and Silk Crochet buttons; collar trimmed in same manner; 30 in. long; worth every cent of $10

We positively **retail at wholesale prices,** and that for which we ask **$5, $10, $15 or $20** you could not buy at any retail store in America for less than $8 to $35. A cloak equal to our make cannot be bought *anywhere at any price.* Ours retain their shape, they look as fresh and bright after a season's wear as the very first day they were put on. Thousands of ladies order our cloaks by mail each season. We want you as a customer also. Why not send for one of these *fine cloaks at $6, $7.50 or $10,* and our **special cloak and fur catalogue,** showing a hundred other styles, each one distinct in itself, each one a masterpiece, and each one about **half** regular retail price. You run no risk whatever you do. Any reason for the return of a garment is sufficient. Your money will be cheerfully refunded.
Samples of cloth and plush upon application.

EDWARD B. GROSSMAN & CO
178 STATE ST.
CHICAGO
Exclusive Cloak and Fur House

Dress Shields

should be worn by all bicycle riders, as they contain no rubber, are light, white, odorless and waterproof. Made of a natural fibre without the use of chemicals, and they last twice as long as others.

SOLD EVERYWHERE
Sample Pair sent on receipt of 25 cents (stamps)

THE OMO MANUFACTURING CO.
67 New Street, New York

HAVE YOU EVER been tempted to look beautiful? WOODBURY'S FACIAL SOAP will do what your looking-glass has often said could not be done. It is a skin beautifier. Send for book and sample.

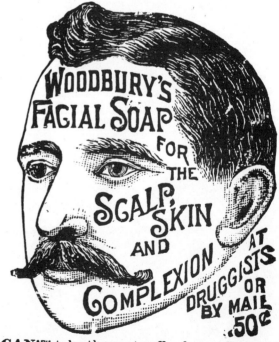

I CAN'T take the spots off a frog. Soap was not invented for that purpose, but WOODBURY'S FACIAL SOAP will make the human skin most beautiful to look upon. At druggists', or by mail, 50c.

THE JENNESS-MILLER
MODEL BODICE

DESIGNED BY ANNIE JENNESS-MILLER

A Perfect Corset Substitute.

The Model Bodice was designed to meet the wants of that very large class of women who are still wedded to the corset idea. It is graceful in shape, comfortable in fit, and suggestive of the corset in general style, while absolutely free from its objections. Many who have accepted the bodice as a substitute for the corset are loud in its praise, for getting rid of the corset steel often means freedom from suffering.

New York, Feb. 6, '90.   ANNIE JENNESS MILLER.

The Model Bodice is manufactured with every possible care, in three qualities, in White and Black material, and is boned with **Genuine Whalebone.** The yokes are trimmed on neck and arm-scye with torchon lace on the white goods, and black silk trimming on the black goods. A ribbon is run through the trimming, and gives a dainty finish, besides providing a means of making the yoke set neatly around the neck. In the body the bones are judiciously arranged to make it fit smoothly.

Sizes kept in stock are [20 waist, 30 bust] to and including [32 waist, 42 bust].

Style 701	Regular Length	[8 in. U. A.]	White American Coutil, Bone Buttons,	$1 75
" 701	Long Waist	[9 in. U. A.]	" " " "	2 00
" 710	Regular Length	[8 in. U. A.]	" Fine Jean, Pearl "	2 25
" 710	Long Waist	[9 in. U. A.]	" " " "	2 50
" 710B	Regular Length	[8 in. U. A.]	Black, " " Ivory "	2 75
" 710B	Long Waist	[9 in. U. A.]	" " " "	3 00

Send snug waist measure taken over dress, and we will send the proper size.

Bodices will be sent by mail, postage prepaid, on receipt of price, and money refunded if they are not satisfactory. They are probably sold in your town, but to save trouble of inquiring, send us your address, and our catalogue will tell you who has them. Illustrated catalogue mailed free to any address.

GEO. FROST & CO., 31 BEDFORD ST., BOSTON, MASS.

KIRK'S JUVENILE

TOILET SOAP
EFFECTIVE   PURE
    DELICATE   FRAGRANT

FASHIONABLE
Fur Neck Boas.

Mink, with head and tail, $5, $7, $10, and $15 for the very best. Hudson Bay Sable Boas, $15, $25, $30. and $35 for the best. Persian Lamb, $5, $7 and $9. Gray Krimmer, $5. Also Boas of other Furs, $2.50, $3, $4, $5, and $6. Muffs to match, at correspondingly low prices. Large stock of Sealskin Garments, and all Fashionable Furs of every description.

Fashion Book mailed free.

C. C. SHAYNÉ, Manufacturer,
124 W. 42d St.,
Near 6th Avenue L Station.

FACE TO FACE.

The pleasure of a confidential chat is doubled by the sweet breath that goes with a well-ordered system. And that is always insured by

Ripans Tabules.

Sweet breath, bright eye,
        clear complexion.

Ripans Tabules.

Boy's Splendid Outfit $2.98.

Sizes 4 to 14 Years. Postage 40c. Extra.

SPECIAL.

From Aug. 23d until Sept. 23d we offer this Special Outfit consisting of **Complete Double-Breasted Suit, Extra Pair Pants and Oxford Hat** at

$2.98.

These are made from a "Basket Woven" heavy-weight wool Cheviot in Gray and Brown shades. Pants have

Double Seat, Double Knees and Duplex Pocket.

The Outfit is guaranteed equal to any Outfit sold in this country for $5.00. We will fill all orders received up to September 23d at the SPECIAL PRICE $2.98. Money refunded unless perfectly satisfactory.

Note. Our Establishment is the largest in New York; Mail-Order System the most perfect in America. Send your name NOW for our list of September Bargains. Ready September 1st. Mailed FREE to any address.

BLOOMINGDALE BROS.,
Third Ave., 59th and 60th Sts., NEW YORK.

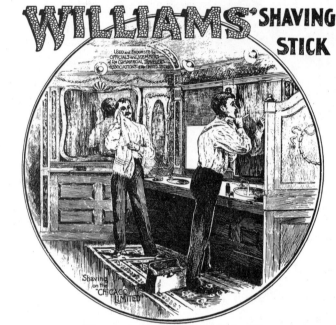
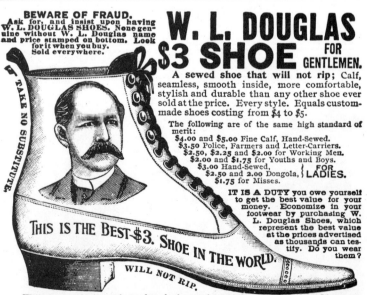

School Dress.
SPECIAL.

SCHOOL DRESS of handsome All-Wool Plaids and Stripes trimmed with braid and lined throughout; style exactly as shown in cut :—

6, 8 and 10 yrs. at

$2.79.

12 and 14 yrs. at

$2.95.

Better value has never been offered. NOTE. Our Establishment is the largest in New York; Mail - Order System the most perfect in America.

Our 48-page Illustrated Catalogue of IMPORTANT SPECIAL VALUES will be MAILED FREE upon request. Write for a copy.

BLOOMINGDALE BROS.,
Third Ave., 59th & 60th Sts., New York.

He won't be happy till he gets it!

PEAR'S

SCRAMBLING FOR IT.

Here is a good-natured tussle for a cake of Pears' Soap, which only illustrates how necessary it becomes to all people who have once tried it and discovered its merits. Some who ask for it have to contend for it in a more serious way, and that too in drug stores, where all sorts of vile and inferior soaps, represented as "just as good," are urged upon them as substitutes. But there is nothing "just as good," and they can always get the genuine Pears' Soap if they will be as persistent as are these urchins.

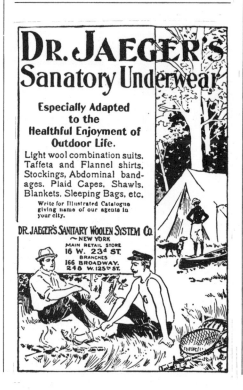

FOR PIMPLES
USE
Cuticura SOAP

THE ONLY
PREVENTIVE
OF
PIMPLES

Because the only preventive of clogging, inflammation, and irritation of the pores, the CAUSE of pimples, blackheads, blotches, rough, red, oily skin, baby blemishes and falling hair

N. B.—CUTICURA SOAP is not only the most effective skin purifying and beautifying soap in the world, but the purest and sweetest for toilet, bath, and nursery.

W.B.Corsets

Fit well.
Look well.
Wear well.

Made with 4, 5, and 6 hook clasps — short, medium, long, and extra long waists. $1.00 to $5.00 per pair, at all retailers. If your dealer does not keep them, write to W. B., 62 Walker St., New York.

FREE Send stamp for set of *W. B. Sachets*, assorted odors. Dainty, lasting perfume.

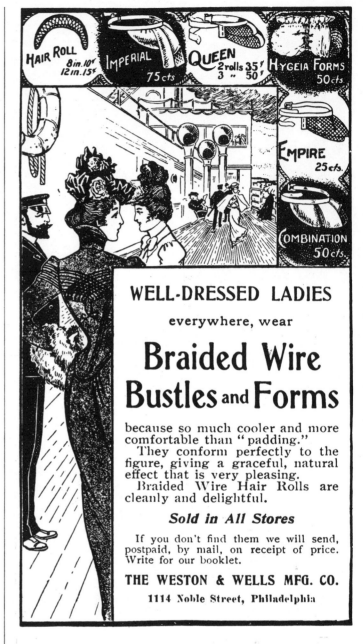

HAIR ROLL 8 in. 10¢ 12 in. 15¢ — IMPERIAL 75 cts — QUEEN 2 rolls 35¢ 3 " 50¢ — HYGEIA FORMS 50 cts — EMPIRE 25 cts — COMBINATION 50 cts

WELL-DRESSED LADIES

everywhere, wear

Braided Wire
Bustles and Forms

because so much cooler and more comfortable than "padding."
They conform perfectly to the figure, giving a graceful, natural effect that is very pleasing.
Braided Wire Hair Rolls are cleanly and delightful.

Sold in All Stores

If you don't find them we will send, postpaid, by mail, on receipt of price. Write for our booklet.

THE WESTON & WELLS MFG. CO.
1114 Noble Street, Philadelphia

Improved Breast Support

By its use the weight of the breasts is removed from the dress waist to the shoulders, giving **coolness and dress comfort**, ventilation, a perfect shape bust and free and easy movement of the body. Made with skirt and hose supporter attachments. **All deficiency of development supplied.** When ordering send bust measure.

Sizes from 30 to 38......$1.00
"   "   40 " 45...... 1.25
"   over 45   ...... 1.50

Agents Wanted

MRS. C. D. NEWELL, 223 Dickey Ave., Chicago

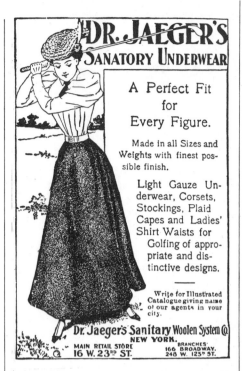

WILLIAMS'

SHAVING SOAPS

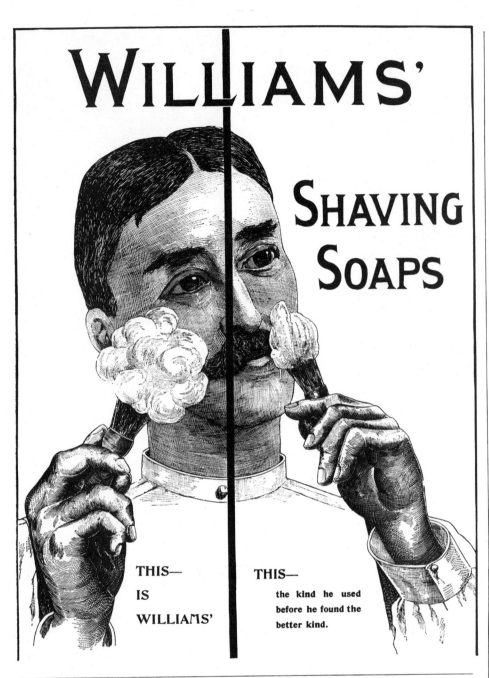

THIS—
IS
WILLIAMS'

THIS—
the kind he used
before he found the
better kind.

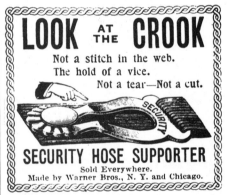

W.B. AMERICA'S LEADING CORSETS

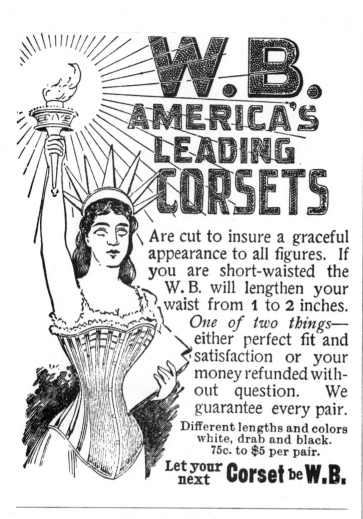

Are cut to insure a graceful appearance to all figures. If you are short-waisted the W.B. will lengthen your waist from **1** to **2** inches. *One of two things*—either perfect fit and satisfaction or your money refunded without question. We guarantee every pair.

Different lengths and colors white, drab and black. 75c. to $5 per pair.

Let your next Corset be W.B.

LADIES secure a beautiful complexion by using the Bon-Ton Face Steamer, which removes tan, freckles, pimples and wrinkles. Any lady can steam her own face. Lady agents wanted in every city in the U.S. and Canada. Send $3 to the Bon-Ton Face Steamer Co., 2240 Glenwood Ave., Toledo, O., and we will send you prepaid, one Bon-Ton Steamer.

PAT: APPLED FOR.

Glove = Fitting Bicycle Leggins

$1.50 **JERSEY** of finest quality made. Conforms to every movement and **is the only really satisfactory Bicycle Leggin for Ladies'** wear. Black, blue, tan, dark and cadet gray. Kept in all sizes. With price, send measure of ankle, calf, and below knee, length of leggin and size of shoe. Expressed unless 10 cents is sent for mailing.

SMITH & BYRON, 146 5th Avenue, Chicago, Ill.

Improved DEWEY ACME Corset and Dress Protector

A COMPLETE GARMENT which can be worn under the corset or flannels, protecting the clothing from perspiration. **Better and Cheaper** than dress shields, one pair doing the work of six.

Bust measure, 28–33, **$.80**
"   "   34–39, **1.00**
"   "   40–46, **1.25**

Send money by Post Office Order. Catalogue Free.

AGENTS WANTED.

M. DEWEY, Mfr.
1397 West Monroe Street, Chicago

NO NEED TO WEAR BLOOMERS

Use PETERSON'S BICYCLE SKIRT HOLDERS

Keeps the skirt from creeping and blowing up. Invisible and adjustable. Comfortable to wear. No need to detach from skirt when walking. For sale by cycle dealers or sent prepaid on receipt of 50 cents. **Agents Wanted.**

H. S. PETERSON & CO.
114 Clark St.,   **Chicago, Ill.**

A SHAMPOO WITH Cuticura SOAP

A warm shampoo with CUTICURA SOAP, followed by gentle applications of CUTICURA, the great skin cure, will clear the scalp of crusts, scales, and dandruff, allay itching, soothe irritation, stimulate the hair follicles, and produce a clean, healthy scalp and luxuriant hair, when all else fails.

LADIES ARE ASSURED

that to cleanse, purify, and beautify the skin, to allay itching and irritation, to heal chafings, excoriations, and ulcerative weaknesses, to speedily cure the first symptoms of torturing, disfiguring skin humors, nothing so pure, so sweet, so wholesome, so speedily effective as warm baths with CUTICURA SOAP, followed, when necessary, by mild applications of CUTICURA (ointment), the great skin cure.

Sold throughout the world. POTTER DRUG AND CHEMICAL CORPORATION, Sole Proprietors, Boston, U. S. A. British depot: F. NEWBERY & SONS, 1, King Edward-st., London, E. C.

Of all the dainty toilet wares
There is to me no soap like Pears'
...ill for aye its patron be
And praise its matchless purity.

Pears' Soap

must always continue to hold its place in the good opinion of women who wish to be beautiful and attractive. Its purity is such that it may be used on the tenderest and most sensitive skin, even that of a new-born babe.

(Established over 100 years—20 International Awards.   Be sure you get the genuine.)

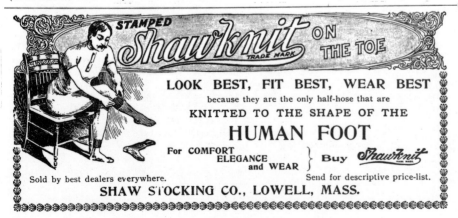

STAMPED Shawknit ON THE TOE

LOOK BEST, FIT BEST, WEAR BEST

because they are the only half-hose that are

KNITTED TO THE SHAPE OF THE

HUMAN FOOT

For COMFORT
ELEGANCE and WEAR } Buy *Shawknit*

Sold by best dealers everywhere.

Send for descriptive price-list.

SHAW STOCKING CO., LOWELL, MASS.

2 FOR 25¢

LAKEWOOD	3¼ IN	LACONIA	2¼ IN
OPORTO	2¾ IN	ESSEX	2 IN
OTISCO	2¼ IN	CHANDOS	2¼ IN

Collars Differ! Why?

Because the essence of good workmanship is brains. We use brains as well as other material in making our collars. All collars are not alike, because the brains and other material differ. We make Collars and Cuffs exclusively, and our sixty years' experience will benefit you. Learn a lesson by buying the **Corliss-Coon** Collars, two for 25 cents. Your dealer will supply you. If not, write us, *stating size.* *"Correct Dress" for Various Occasions described in Catalogue, sent free.*
CORLISS, COON & CO., 276-278 Franklin St., Chicago.

This waist is made in black, white and colored taffeta silk, striped with black or white velvet.
—
ORIGINAL DESIGNS IN NEGLIGÉES, LINGERIE AND SHIRT WAISTS.

Chas. T. Jones

1163-5 BROADWAY, N.Y.

Of course it's Pears'

SOURCES

Collier's Weekly
Donahoe's Magazine
Frank Leslie's Illustrated Newspaper
Frank Leslie's Lady's Journal
Gem of the West
Life
Peterson's Magazine
San Francisco Newsletter and Californian Advertiser
Scientific American
The Ladies' Home Journal
The Youth's Companion
Vogue